# HOLINESS
### *in the*
# GOSPELS

# HOLINESS

### *in the*

# GOSPELS

### KENT BROWER

BEACON HILL PRESS
OF KANSAS CITY

Copyright 2005
by Kent Brower and Beacon Hill Press of Kansas City

ISBN 978-0-8341-2191-1

Printed in the
United States of America

Cover Design: Keith Alexander

**Library of Congress Cataloging-in-Publication Data**

Brower, K. E. (Kent E.)
   Holiness in the Gospels / Kent Brower.
      p. cm.
   Includes bibliographical references.
   ISBN 0-8341-2191-3 (pbk.)
   1. Bible. N.T. Gospels—Criticism, interpretation, etc. 2. Holiness—Biblical teaching. I. Title.

   BS2555.6.H6B76 2005
   234'.8'09015—dc22

                                                                                    2005012752

10   9   8   7   6   5   4   3   2

Dedicated to my parents,
Barry and Jean

# CONTENTS

# PREFACE

The need for a fresh understanding of Christian holiness that addresses the 21st-century context is becoming increasingly clear in denominations within the Wesleyan-Holiness tradition, such as the Church of the Nazarene. Without such an articulation and application of this aspect of Christian doctrine, one that is faithful to Scripture and tradition, the raison d'être for these denominations could easily be lost in the morass of competing theological and other considerations. This book examines only a very small part of Scripture; I am very conscious of the privilege of joining in the conversation with people who care deeply about these matters.

In addition to countless scholars who have influenced me over the years, only some of whose names are included in the bibliography, I gratefully acknowledge the contributions of colleagues and students in the M.A. course in Aspects of Christian Holiness at NTC-Manchester. They have influenced almost every line of the book. Their lively interaction for well over a decade in which I have had the privilege of teaching on this course highlighted the need for this brief study. The January 2004 intensive class at NTS on Holiness in the Gospels gave me an opportunity to learn from another group of students. They interacted enthusiastically with an earlier form of this book.

The book itself is a slight revision and expansion of the 2000 Collins Holiness Lectures delivered at Canadian Nazarene University College in Calgary, Alberta. Long before I was a student there in the mid-1960s, the faculty at this college realized the importance for the college and the Church of the Nazarene of a lecture series devoted specifically to the topic of Christian holiness. It was an honor to be invited to deliver a series in the college where I was a student and a sometime lecturer. The invitation gave me the opportunity to give sustained attention to the theme. I am also grateful to my own college for its generous sabbatical leave policy, which gave me the time necessary to bring these ideas to a somewhat coherent form.

The most poignant aspect of the visit to Calgary was the fact that my mum and dad were able to attend all of the lectures. Six months later my mother passed away. My dad taught me about Christian holiness as a questioning teenager. I still find myself in agreement with the central points he made. My mother never talked about Christian holiness; she just lived it.

Kent Brower
Nazarene Theological College
Manchester
2004

# INTRODUCTION
## HOLINESS TODAY

◆

## 1. A PASSION FOR HOLINESS

In the modern western Canadian city where the lectures on which this book is based were delivered, there is a theme park that recalls the early days in Alberta. Many people are delighted that it is there. For a minority who look with nostalgia to "the good old days," the theme park has great interest. Life was simpler and communities were stronger. People cared more for each other—you could leave your doors unlocked.

Everything in the theme park is needed within the modern city. Everyone still needs a house in the winter but much prefer well-insulated, centrally heated homes to a draughty, damp house with a coal fire on an open hearth or a wood-burning fire place, however cheery they might seem to be in old photos. Everyone needs streetlights to go on at dusk, but they would rather have a photoelectric cell turn on the lights than to depend upon a lamplighter. And no one wants to return to a time when infant mortality was high and it was very rare for married couples to live to celebrate 50th wedding anniversaries.

Is there a future for the doctrine of Christian holiness in the churches of the 21st century, or will it become a heritage theme park for the denominations that are part of the Holiness Movement? Some have suggested that the doctrine has been all but extinguished in these denominations.[1] Among a plethora of signs noted is the virtual disappearance of the language of "second blessing holiness" and the equally worrying appropriation by the modern charismatic movement in its variety of guises of the language of "baptism with the Spirit." When used, the language has either been emptied of meaning or its connotation has changed.

This lamentable decline of Holiness teaching in the Holiness Movement is partly attributable, some suggest, to spiritual leaders who lost their nerve in the face of changing theological fashion and modern biblical criticism. If the doctrine were ever to be revived, some argued, it would only be with a reaffirmation of the indissoluble connection between Christian holiness and a definite, once-for-all-time, crisis experience of entire sanctification through the baptism of the Holy Spirit. In one denomination in the Holiness Movement, there is more than a little anxiety about a decline in the church's understanding of holiness.[2] In response, some leaders urge greater conformity to a particular form of words focusing on the language of "secondness." They believe that the way to maintain loyalty to Holiness teaching is to reinforce the particular formulation of Christian holiness associated with the American 19th-century Holiness Movement. Others of a more Wesleyan orientation are less concerned about words or sequence than they are about essence. For them the life of holiness is more important than the description of "the experience."

Much of the time, of course, the laity really aren't particularly bothered. If they come to a Holiness Movement denomination from outside the tradition, it is rarely on the basis of theological conviction or experience. And, once in the church, they are likely to receive a rather minimal introduction with little emphasis upon terminology and even less upon the experience the terminology describes. As long as the congregation has a warm fellowship and the worship is to their taste, and provided that the sermons are not too long or too challenging, they are happy. If not, they will soon move on to another church of any denomination provided it is more user-friendly for them as consumers. The substance of the doctrine has thereby gone by default.

For others who grew up in the Holiness Movement denominations, the theme of Christian holiness is not particularly galvanizing. There may be many reasons for this. Some have come to see the whole notion of holiness as rigid and legalistic, leading to a routine and joyless life, centered on churches with a casual and impoverished worship. For some, it has become little more than a shibboleth—a sort of password on the way to ordination but rarely preached persuasively or with conviction. For college students, as it is at NTC-Manchester, it may be the title of a compulsory course for graduation. From the lay perspective, all too often the credibility gap between doctrine and life, noted years ago by Professor Mildred Bangs Wynkoop,[3] remains stubbornly wide.

At the same time, to the extent that our evangelical brothers and sisters pay any attention at all, our teaching on holiness has been caricatured as "sinless perfection." To be honest, some Holiness Movement preachers and people may have given unwitting support to the caricature. But this has always been rejected by serious Holiness thinkers as an odious distortion of Scripture and experience. Alternatively, the message itself may be submerged in the sticky morass of mildly Reformed and decidedly fundamentalistic popular evangelicalism that dominates the conservative Christian constituency and affects great swaths of the laity within Holiness Movement denominations.

There is a great deal of substance to this description of the current malaise within the Holiness Movement. Ironically, however, just as traditional "Holiness" teaching is coming upon hard times in parts of the Holiness Movement, a concern for holiness is emerging on the agenda of other parts of the Christian community.[4] The 20th century has seen the rise of Pentecostalism,[5] and the charismatic renewal has affected all of Western Christianity and beyond. To some in the Holiness Movement, the charismatic renewal with its life and vigor has proved to be very attractive. Its emphasis on power, joy, ecstasy, and the gifts of the Spirit has come as a challenge to that which seems dull by comparison. Others, longing for a sense of the holy, are looking again at the liturgical riches of the Christian church,[6] including a new and healthy appreciation for the Orthodox faith[7] with its sense of the mystery of the Holy and its understanding of the Holy Trinity.[8] "Holiness" is back on the Christian agenda.

The charismatic movement, of course, is easy prey to the postmodern elevation of the nonrational. Noncognitive experience becomes the norm[9] leading to the perpetual and restless search for the novel and the spectacular. The strong anti-intellectual streak in Pentecostalism (often shared by its Holiness Movement cousins) means that interest in theology has been somewhat delayed.[10] All that is changing. A growing number of charismatics are concerned to understand the theological basis for their experiences, realizing that the need to avoid the ever-present danger of spurious experience requires good theology. Hence, this engagement in the task of theology by those in the charismatic renewal (and its noncharismatic admirers)[11] is to be warmly welcomed not least because of the contribution it could well make to the rest of the Church.

But what about the Holiness Movement? Is this bleak prospect for Holiness teaching in Holiness churches the only one? Definitely not. Among younger scholars and laity alike, there is a growing passion for holiness. From rather limited personal observations, young people are searching for a new vision of holiness, one that is more biblically responsible and theologically coherent than the teaching they heard in the past. Most importantly, they are looking for a vision of holiness that translates into a genuine message of good news through engagement with their contemporary world with all its problems. This, they insist, must be a doctrine that emerges from the text of Scripture, coheres with the cardinal doctrines of the church, is centered in worship, and issues in an obedient faith community. They want to live the holy life in the 21st century not in a 19th-century Holiness theme park.

If this "passion for holiness" is to become more than a passing fancy, it must indeed be founded on Scripture and integrated with the great doctrines of the Church.[12] This book suggests some of the foundations in a small part of Scripture that is sometimes overlooked in our doctrinal discussions. It is not, however, a detailed exegetical study of key Holiness texts. It owes much more to a narrative reading of Scripture on the one hand and the mushrooming conversations on Christian holiness on the other. Perhaps it might be part of that conversation as people in the Holiness Movement try to understand afresh what God's call of a holy people means in the 21st century.[13]

## 2. ASSUMPTIONS IN THIS BOOK

This short book has limitations that will become apparent. The section of material to be covered in each of the Gospels makes no claim whatsoever to be exhaustive or comprehensive. There are also several theological and methodological assumptions that inform the discussion. None of them can be defended at length although it is hoped that what follows confirms their legitimacy. The following brief statements identify some of them.

First, all Christian Holiness *is derived in relation to God, the Holy One.* W. T. Purkiser agrees with most modern scholars when he states, "God alone is holy in himself. All other holiness is derived from a relationship with Him."[14] Things, places, and beings are holy only in relationship to Him. Hartley, following Milgrom and other Old Testament scholars, posits holiness as the "quintessential nature of Yahweh as God."[15] Thus, God's holiness cannot be defined simply by reflecting on the awesomeness of God, the *mysterium tremendum*[16] or the transcendence, otherness, and uniqueness of God[17] or even His purity and abhorrence of sin. God is holy in essence.

Second, holiness *is a theme that runs through the entire Scripture.* The canonical shape of Scripture begins with the holy God who creates and sustains all things. It ends with the holy God in the center of His holy people in the holy place. No part of Holy Scripture has merely antiquarian interest. For example, the Levitical Holiness Code of Leviticus 19—26 and the Old Testament prophets tell us something about how we ought to understand *Christian* holiness. Thus, if Christian holiness *is* a biblical doctrine, it will find expression throughout the entire canon of Scripture. The extent of the theme has been clearly demonstrated by G. J. Thomas, who draws particular attention to the mission of the people of God as His holy people.[18]

Third, *word studies alone cannot identify themes* that run throughout Scripture.[19] The key limitation in word study is that *words gain their meaning from context.*[20] We need, therefore, to pay particularly careful attention to the meaning of words in their original *historical* as well as *literary* context. On the positive side, word study takes seriously the language of the biblical text.[21] But a search for key words like "holiness" and "sanctification" would not take us very far in our attempt to understand Christian holiness in the Gospels. Apart from anything else, the concept of holiness is too big for word study alone. Holiness is people-of-God language, a notion that defines the essential character of the people of God. Therefore the absence of the word does not imply the absence of the thought. Others might start the conversation with exegesis of selected texts. Starting there takes seriously the text of Scripture—but the exegete needs to be aware of what preconceptions are being brought to the text. There is always the danger of "finding what one is looking for" or of using the text as a series of "proof texts."

Fourth, as is being recognized increasingly these days in biblical studies, *doctrinal truth is presented in narrative* every bit as much as in doctrinal or propositional statements. The person of God is revealed by how he or she acts toward the people just as clearly as by any nouns or adjectives attributed to God or His spokesperson. Under the influence of new types of literary criticism, contemporary biblical theology looks at the whole story of God. Narrative approaches to the Gospels have been shown to be particularly illuminating in uncovering a level of meaning that may be obscured through other approaches. "A controlled reading of the gospel[s], which take[s] the intention of the implied author[s] . . . seriously as [composing] . . . first century document[s] addressed to [their] implied reader[s], also in the first century[,] allows modern readers to hear the same message and apply it to their own lives today."[22] We therefore need to take the whole biblical narrative as the resource for developing a coherent understanding of Christian holiness.[23]

Fifth, as well as providing us with our only source of hard historical evidence about Jesus of Nazareth, the *Gospels are theological documents*. The central revelation of God's good purposes comes in Jesus Christ, to whom the Gospel narratives bear witness. The Gospel stories are the vehicles of the evangelists' *theology* as well as their interest in the historical Jesus or their own *Sitz im Leben.*[24]

To be sure, the Gospels tell about the life of Jesus and the disciples *before Pentecost*. This raises an important question. Are the Gospels relevant to the post-Pentecost Church in which we live? At best, it is argued, the disciples are pre-entire sanctification; they are entirely sanctified at Pentecost when they are baptized with the Spirit. When they were with Jesus, the Spirit had not yet been given and it is the Spirit who sanctifies (see John 7:39). At worst they were not even Christians. Because Jesus had not yet been crucified, Pentecost was the point of their initial salvation.

Although one should not underestimate the significant changes that the Resurrection, Ascension, and Pentecost make for the disciples, one should not diminish the importance of their time with Jesus either. In the following chapters, the experience of the disciples with Jesus, "son of Adam, son of God" (Luke 3:38), God's Holy One in the midst of His disciples, is shown to be relevant indeed. The disciples are connected to the source of holiness. The change between pre- and post-Pentecost has more to do with the extent of the Spirit's presence both in terms of ethnic diversity and all-pervasiveness than it has to do with a qualitative difference between being with the Holy One [Jesus] and being filled with the Holy Spirit. These disciples now knew that Jesus, the Crucified One, was indeed the Jewish Messiah. The Messiah was not "restoring the kingdom to Israel" in any sense that they might previously have wished. Their ethnocentric understanding of God's big purposes and their own political ambitions were at once too narrow and self-centered. Rather, He was the Messiah for all people. They came to see that God's purposes for Israel as a light to the nations came to rest upon Jesus. This was no easy change for them—we only have to listen to Peter's struggles in Acts 9—10 as he comes to terms with Gentile believers!

Another major obstacle to seeing holiness in the Gospels is a static view of salvation formalized as justification/sanctification. These terms and their meaning are vital to Christian theology. But since these terms rarely appear in the Gospels, it is argued that the *story* of Jesus and the disciples can be safely ignored on matters concerning salvation. We need Paul, it is argued, to talk about salvation, and in Paul's view that is exclusively a matter of Jesus' death, or, possibly, His death and resurrection. Salvation cannot be reduced to terms that can become static, however, because salvation is dynamic.

Sixth, holiness is *an incarnational issue.* Holiness teaching is rooted in the incarnation of Christ. Important though Christian experience is as "the point at which theology is grounded in history," experience "must be grounded in the existence of something which is independent of the experience itself."[25] It must be grounded in Christ. The fact is that we see the holiness of God most clearly in the incarnation of the Son of God. Our salvation, centered in the cross of Christ, must also be understood within the context of the Incarnation, for if Jesus were not God, He could not do anything about our condition; and if He were not fully human in every respect, He would know nothing about our condition. Our doctrine of the Incarnation, then, is central to our soteriology. The doctrine of Christian holiness is but one aspect of the doctrine of the Incarnation. The fully God/fully human tension in the Incarnation must never be reduced by ignoring either of its dimensions.

The final assumption is that holiness is *a Trinitarian issue.* That may seem like a truism,[26] but its implications are far-reaching. Trinitarian language, of course, is rarely explicitly used. The evangelists use essentially functional language. But our ontological use is a legitimate extension of their language. This will become rather more important when we look at the Gospel of John. Suffice it to say at this point that a Trinitarian view of God underlies the entire holiness motif even when it is not on the surface.[27]

## 3. FROM LUKE TO MATTHEW: THE STRUCTURE OF THIS BOOK

A word of explanation about the plan of this book may be helpful. In chapter 1, a brief outline of the quest for holiness in the second Temple period will establish the backdrop against which we need to read the Gospels. The Gospels are first read in the Greco-Roman world. But the story they tell has its roots deep in the Palestinian Judaism of the second Temple period. We really only understand Jesus and His disciples when we remember that they are Jews in occupied Judea and Galilee.

This is followed by the Gospel of Luke. The decision to begin with Luke might appear to some to be merely eccentric. Clearly, it has nothing to do with chronology; scholars consider Luke the last of the Synoptic Gospels. Nor is it simplicity; the two-volume Luke-Acts is anything but simple, as the range of current scholarly activity centered on Luke-Acts will attest. Preachers within the Holiness, Pentecostal, and charismatic traditions all consider it to be very important. They look especially to Acts as the warrant for terms like "personal Pentecost," "second blessing," "baptism with the Spirit," "third work of grace," or "signs and wonders."[28]

The reason is rather more simple. We are starting with Christology—the humanity of Jesus as emphasized in Luke followed by His divinity in John's Gospel. Luke helps us with two questions in particular. First, Luke is widely regarded as the Gospel that most emphasizes the Spirit. He also draws out aspects of Jesus' humanity in a helpful way and shows that He conducts His mission in the power of the Spirit. To what extent does the relationship between Jesus and the Spirit help us understand the life of believers? Second, Jesus' ministry often brings Him into conflict with that other holiness movement, the Pharisees. How does Jesus define holiness? And what does holiness look like for the new people of God? These questions receive attention in Luke's Gospel, although not only in his Gospel.

If the emphasis in chapter 2 is on Jesus' humanity, chapter 3 moves to the other aspect of Christology, the divinity of Jesus. Here attention is directed specifically to the invitation of Jesus' disciples to share the mutual indwelling of Father and Son as shown in the Gospel of John. The notion of mutuality is touched upon in a short section on the Trinity, a section that is simple enough for nonspecialists to understand while faithful to solid modern theological scholarship. Then the implications of humanity's creation in God's image are drawn out ever so briefly. These are deep waters indeed but perhaps John can tell us something about the privileges and responsibilities that come with this mutual indwelling.

In chapter 4, we look at the journey of Jesus with His disciples through the whole of Mark's Gospel. Mark's Gospel, the first Gospel, is a masterpiece of deceptively simple narration. Although its primary theme is directed to understanding who Jesus is as Messiah, Son of God, Mark also gives us a great deal of help in understanding discipleship. If the life of holiness is anything like a journey, perhaps this Gospel can offer some clues about its features.

While chapter 4 looks at the whole Gospel of Mark, chapter 5 concentrates on a small section of Matthew. The well-known teaching of Jesus, "Be perfect, therefore, as your heavenly Father is perfect" (Matt. 5:48), is the centerpiece of this study. Is this just an impossible dream or a present reality?

Of course, anyone who sets out to examine the scriptural basis for any aspect of Christian doctrine within the confines of a short book must acknowledge at the outset that the coverage will be, at best, highly selective. I have, therefore, set myself a much more modest goal, reflected in the original title of the lectures, *Aspects of Holiness in the Gospels.* Even with that limitation, the best that can be achieved is a brief look at selected highlights. Others will no doubt wish to say more in due course on this subject.

# 1

# HOLINESS IN THE
# SECOND TEMPLE PERIOD

◆

## 1. HOLINESS IN THE GRECO-ROMAN WORLD

In the initial phases of Christian expansion into the Greco-Roman world, the followers of Jesus were predominantly Jews and the story of Jesus was first proclaimed in Jewish synagogues. Fierce debate, perhaps even leading to violence, may have taken place as the messianic Jews disputed with their fellows about Jesus the Messiah.[29] Of course Jesus and the first disciples lived within the confines of second Temple Judaism. But the world in which the gospel of the kingdom of God was proclaimed soon moved outside these boundaries. It is in this context that the gospel needed to take root and thrive.

Before the end of the first Christian century, it is likely that the Gospels themselves were being read widely across the Eastern Mediterranean.[30] "The Gospels have a historical context," writes Bauckham, "but that context is not the evangelist's community. It is the early Christian movement at the end of the first century."[31] The Gospels, then, have a setting that can be described in general terms as the Greco-Roman world. This is the cultural milieu in which any notion of holiness made its way and the context in which the first readers lived their lives. Although a full discussion of the Greco-Roman context would not advance our understanding of holiness in the Gospels very much, a few salient features are worth noting,[32] if only to remind ourselves that the reception of the gospel always has a context that colors what is heard.

First, religion was everywhere and highly visible. Various religious practices dominated all aspects of life from civic and public office to private rites of passage like birth and death. Tem-

ples and shrines commanded public space. Images were prominent because divine figures needed an image. Many highly visible ceremonies took place. Indeed, probably an "overwhelming
number of all public events were explicitly religious in character."[33] Meals, for instance, had religious connotations because the
general populace believed that the gods were active and devotion to them worked. So many social meals were held in honor
of a god. The god in whose honor the meal was given was
thought to be presiding and present. Meals were joyous social
occasions with no tension between social and religious character, even in Christianity.

Second, people took a very open-minded approach to new
religious traditions. Instead of competitors, these new religions
were simply added to the portfolio of religions followed by the
worshipers without any sense that the devotees were bringing dishonor to their own gods. Gentiles, therefore, would come to synagogue without sensing any need to give up other associations.

Jews, by contrast, faced the tension between their theological distinctives and their wider cultural context. These distinctives, based upon their key identity markers of circumcision,
food rules, and Sabbath observance, tended to make them separate from their Gentile neighbors. They did not have images, and
they were devoted exclusively to God. Hurtado comments, "Devout Jews saw their religious commitments and traditions as distinctive and characteristically held themselves aloof from much
of the religious life of the larger Roman world."[34] The same im-
ageless monotheism was the pattern of the early Christians.

Third, the exercise of power was the closest Greco-Roman
popular piety came to a notion of holiness. Power was seen in
nature. Thus, the gods were feared and worshiped. But they had
little if anything to do with ethical goodness.[35] They were almost
never described as holy. At a philosophical level, by contrast, the
divine sphere was an absolute, intellectual principle completely
separate from the world. Similar concepts were used by the Hel-
lenistic Jewish writer Philo, who described God as "pure being."
For Philo, there was also a divine principle or condition of "the

Good," a term used to characterize Israel's God.[36] Harrington notes that in Philo "God is perfect because he is transcendent and above human comprehension."[37] But holiness, per se, was not a major concern.

Fourth, temples were crucial. "People frequented them for a range of purposes and combined social and religious life and activities easily within their precincts."[38] Mount Olympus was thought to be the meeting place of the gods and the link between heaven and earth.[39] Priests as a class of people were generally highly regarded.[40] They were a sort of "walking temple" who took on the inviolability of the shrine.[41] Because the Greco-Roman religions rarely had sacred texts, the idea of a divine law such as the Torah was quite alien. The laws of nature were supreme.[42] There was little understanding of a concept of sacred books.[43] The priests, thus, assumed a pivotal role as ritual experts and mediators between humanity and the divine. Although temples were sacred sites, no one used the term "holy land" except Israel. The closest one comes to a link between holiness and the land in the Greco-Roman world was the importance of festivals tied to the agricultural cycle.[44] Nor did any people consider themselves to be a holy people outside of the Judeo-Christian tradition.[45]

Fifth, ritual rather than any belief or creed was the primary cultic focus. Interestingly enough, ritual purity was essential for participation in the rites of a god. Those who were defiled were prohibited from worship. Generally, impurity was connected in some way with bodily functions such as birth, intercourse, or death.[46] But ritual purification could be achieved usually through use of water or blood as part of some festivals.

This scarcely does justice to the wide variety of practices that face the Jesus movement in the Greco-Roman world. Suffice it to say that the notions of impurity and purification in Judaism had certain affinities with other practices. The differences are pronounced, however. A god who called his people to be a holy people living lives that reflect his holiness would not find a ready connection with the general views of this period. In contrast to the Jewish and early Christian notions, ethical holiness was rarely an issue in Greco-Roman religion—the gods themselves were just not interested in ethical purity.

## 2. HOLINESS IN SECOND TEMPLE JUDAISM

We can only really understand holiness in the Gospels if we take seriously the historical context in which the New Testament is given birth and in which the Old Testament functioned as the scripture of the people of God. It follows that there are aspects of the practices, beliefs, and hopes of second Temple Judaism[47] that are important for our understanding. This promises to be much more fruitful for our purposes.

Although there was a variety of Jewish beliefs in the period from 167 B.C. to A.D. 70, all strands of Judaism agreed on the fundamentals. Roughly speaking, the religious worldview of second Temple Judaism might be summarized something like this. First, *God* was *the holy, creator God.* Holiness was more than one of His attributes: it was His quintessential nature.[48] He alone was holy: humans, places, or objects were only holy insofar as they were related to the source of holiness.[49] Holiness, then, could not be divorced from relationship with the Holy One. To put it another way, *the holiness of places, things, and people was always a derived holiness.*

As a consequence of God's holiness, *the people were called to be holy,* a kingdom of priests and a holy nation, God's own people in the world and in a special *relationship* with Him. He would be their God, the Holy One living in their midst. He himself would provide the means whereby He might safely dwell with them and make a way for them to keep in covenant relationship with Him. As the source of all holiness, being near God was an essential requirement for holiness. This might be understood in physical terms. Ancient Israel had structured its camp and tabernacle in such a way as to guard God's people from the danger of God's holiness.[50] The holy of holies in the Temple still retained that sanctity. The people, in turn, were to develop characteristics like God himself that would affect every dimension of life.[51] "Thus, a fundamental feature of the Judaism in which Jesus was nurtured was the option of a radical pursuit of holiness."[52]

The call to be a holy people required *separation*. The people were called out from the other nations and saw themselves as God's own people. But this was not all. Some argue that, even in Israel, this was far more than mere separation from the nations. Rather, "faithfulness, love, justice, honesty, kindness and purity emerge as aspects of divine holiness that are to be replicated by the people of God."[53] As soon as Israel began to see its separateness as an end in itself, the people's holiness became a barrier rather than a means to God's mission in the world.[54] This became the key issue for the holiness movements of the second Temple period and the essential point of divergence between Jesus and the other holiness movements, as will be shown later. But *separation was never intended to be an end in itself.*[55]

Second, the concept of *election* was the foundation stone of their self-understanding. Israel believed that God had chosen them and they were His covenant people. This choice was completely unexpected and unmerited. God delivered them by His mighty hand from the oppression of Egypt and called them to enter into a gracious covenant with himself. The call of God was primarily *directed to a people, not to individuals.* They were to be His holy people as a holy people—together.[56] The notion of a holy people, a covenant community, is fundamental to understanding Israel. As a people, Israel was God's chosen people to bring justice, wisdom, and peace to the whole created order. Sadly, this was not currently happening. Israel was a subjugated people.

Third, *God has always been faithful* to His covenant promises; alas, the same could not be said for the people. Their covenant unfaithfulness led ultimately to exile. But even while they were in exile, God was faithful and promised the people that if they returned to Him, He would restore them to be His holy people and would dwell in their midst again in the Holy Land. A remnant did indeed return, but the restoration had been neither as glorious nor as complete as the pictures painted by the prophets suggested it would be. Although they again lived in the land, *the covenant people of God were,* in a spiritual sense, *still in exile,* still awaiting God's promised deliverance, still longing for the fullness of the return.[57] The present evil age, including subjugation to the Roman Empire, was a daily reality. The longed-for age to come had not arrived. But why?

This could not be a matter of God's unfaithfulness—rather, the people needed to repent, the nation needed to return to full covenant faithfulness, and the land needed to be cleansed. To be sure, on the one hand the people realized that their plight was not merely of human dimension. Supramundane forces of evil were aligned against their God. But that was only part of the answer. Their present condition could only be because Israel in some sense was still in its sin. That was why the future was yet to be realized. What was needed now was loyalty to the covenant, even in the face of opposition, whether human or spiritual. They needed to demonstrate membership in the true people of God through ever more faithful obedience to the covenant.[58] Then God would come, defeat His (and their) enemies, and establish His reign as promised. How this would be done was given a variety of answers: the sectarian community at Qumran and the Pharisees were only two of the holiness/renewal movements in the second Temple period.

Included in God's promises was *the hope of a new in-the-heart covenant* with His people. This would not be like the old covenant, which they had failed to keep. Rather, it would enable them to be a holy people in a new way.[59] He would also cleanse and renew the holy place. Then the holy God could again dwell in their midst, the nations would come to worship God in Jerusalem, the center of the Holy Land.[60]

But that was all *in the future.* There was little sense that the current state of affairs was the complete fulfillment of the promises of God. How could they be when the Romans still ruled and when the Gentiles profaned God's name and despised His people? The land itself was impure, polluted by the presence of the Gentiles who did not follow the Torah.

Inextricably linked to this substructure of belief was the institutional framework of second Temple Judaism. At the center stood the Temple; its importance can hardly be exaggerated. It was the focal point of every aspect of Jewish life. Although some people rejected the Jerusalem Temple because of its corrupt current leadership, most thought of it as the dwelling place of God, with the holy of holies being the symbolic *locus of the presence of God.*

The Temple was also the *place for sacrifice* leading to forgiveness of sins and cleansing from defilement. Two daily offerings were offered to celebrate the presence of God: burnt offerings for the deity and peace offerings to be eaten by the people. Two different offerings were made to restore the worshiper to fellowship after sin or impurity: the sin offering [*hatta't*] both for sin and impurity (which were not the same thing) and the guilt offering—a kind of sin offering made as restitution to God for a specific wrong. The Temple was also the place for national or corporate atonement. Passover and the Day of Atonement were the main times of corporate repentance and renewal. Both were centered on the Temple.

Not only was it the center of the sacrificial system, but also it was the *national shrine.* The political significance of the Temple should not be underestimated. This was directly connected to the notion of it as the dwelling place of God. When Israel had a king, he was legitimized through the Temple.[61] It was bound up inextricably with the royal house and with royal aspirations.[62] For this reason, the high priest was a central political as well as religious figure. The fact that the high priest was under the direct authority of the Romans, who kept control of his vestments, only added to the tension within the late second Temple period. Jewish nationalism, the Temple, and Judaism were intertwined in the second Temple period in such a way that it is virtually impossible to discuss the Temple authorities without including the Temple itself. In fact, references in the Gospels to the Temple frequently are a cipher for the religious authorities.[63] In the expressive words of Wright, "The Temple was, in Jesus' day, the central symbol of Judaism, the location of Israel's most characteristic praxis, the topic of some of her most vital stories, the answer to her deepest questions, the subject of some of her most beautiful songs."[64] It was also the center for potential political unrest and intrigue.[65] Judea was effectively a temple-state with Jerusalem at its center. Control of the Temple, therefore, was vital. The destruction of the Temple itself was directly related to the nationalistic direction of Judaism, which ended in the Jewish War of A.D. 66.

If the Temple was a pillar in second Temple Judaism, the Torah was the second.[66] The Torah was more than law. It was the covenant document and contained the *halakah, the way of life.* The life of God's holy people was defined by the Torah. The presence of the holy God could only be safe if His people lived lives that reflected His holiness. The Torah set out for them God's mission and their call to it. It also contained the Temple regulations. There was, therefore, a link between Torah and Temple.[67]

The holiness of the land was a key concern in the second Temple period. The land was currently polluted because it was under the control of Gentiles. Both land and Temple were being defiled by the Romans despite any religious niceties they might have attempted to maintain. Alien cultures defiled as well—the memory of the Seleucids and their desecration of the Temple (see 1 Maccabees) as well as the martyrdom of the Maccabean brothers were etched in the national consciousness. The only hope for the people now was that Yahweh would cleanse the land to make it fit again for His people. Many longed for God to raise up a new David or a new Maccabean who would drive the Romans into the sea.

The importance of the Temple and its sanctity cannot, therefore, be exaggerated. Purity and holiness were far from peripheral issues. If the holy God were to dwell with His people again, they would need to be holy. "The political program of postexilic Judaism was the permeation of national life by holiness, a program undergirded by the twin institutions of Torah and Temple."[68] The result was "an ethos of resistance to external power and influence grounded in the quest for holiness."[69]

A key aspect of this kind of holiness revolved around ethnic purity: who was a Jew? This led to highlighting various aspects of praxis including food rules, Sabbath observance, and circumcision as key identity markers within both Palestinian and Diaspora Judaism. These became the boundary markers between God's covenant people and the Gentiles. The "works of the law"[70] were more likely to be identity markers rather than a series of steps by which one attained "people of God" status. Wright suggests that they functioned as "present signs of future vindication."[71]

N. T. Wright observes that these beliefs and structures informed and, in turn, were shaped by "the various different movements, political, social and particularly revolutionary, that characterised the period from 167 B.C. to A.D. 70."[72] In particular, the people of Israel longed for a peaceful and settled existence in their land that would reflect God's presence and blessing. But despite the expectation of God's action to put things right, a gulf existed between expectation and reality. "The basis of the eager expectation that fomented discontent and fuelled revolution was not merely frustration with the inequalities of the Roman imperial system, but the fact that this frustration was set within the context of Jewish monotheism, election and eschatology."[73]

Into this context, the message of John and Jesus came like a lightning strike on dry prairie wood. They announced that the day of God's activity had dawned. The exorcisms and healings, the welcoming of the marginalized, the announcement of the Kingdom, even the relentless progress to the Cross—all of these were like a dry wind fanning the small flames of the hopes of Israel. This restoration eschatology[74] with its promise of God's renewed redeeming action for Israel was the cradle of early Christianity. Without an awareness of this context, we will have great difficulty understanding Jesus and the Gospels, and the call to be a holy people will remain a doctrine divorced from its roots.

## 3. The Pharisees and Purity[75]

The Pharisees were an important holiness movement within second Temple Judaism. For casual readers of the Gospels, they are by far the best-known Jewish group during the time of Jesus, even if the picture that emerges only from the Gospels is inevitably truncated. Their origins are somewhat obscure, but they arose sometime during the Maccabean revolt and were very influential in the Hasmonean period (164-163 B.C.E.). Although after 63 B.C. they no longer exercised direct political power and they remained a relatively small portion of society, their influence was significant during the time of Jesus. Some of them seem to have moved in the direction of active violent revolutionary opposition to Roman rule;[76] others concentrated on the study of the Torah. Although it is impossible to show conclusively, it is possible that there was a degree of tension between the activists and passivists within the Pharisees themselves. After the fall of Jerusalem and the destruction of the Temple in the Jewish War of A.D. 66-70, the Pharisaic emphasis on Torah study became the dominant theme of Judaism, and the Pharisaic tradition became essentially mainstream Judaism.

If intensification of holiness was the *goal* of the Pharisees, the *means* centered on Torah observance. In the Torah God set out for His people the way in which they might remain in covenant relationship with Him. Hence, obedience to the Torah was essential. Because God is holy, purity was especially important. Israel was called to be a holy people, and the Pharisees took this seriously. They lived according to the standards of purity required of priests: if God's people were called to be a kingdom of *priests,* then the purity rules for Temple service should be expanded to include the whole of Israel and the whole land. True allegiance to the covenant demanded this intensification of holiness. Only then would Israel be restored to its independent status as God's holy people dwelling in the Holy Land. Although it cannot be proven, their adherence to priestly purity may have been an implicit criticism of the corruption and secularity of the current Temple establishment.

Three areas in particular drew their attention. First, the food rules laid down for priests in Scripture were extended to the lay Pharisaic community. Mealtime became a crucial expression of their solidarity in strict obedience to the commands of God. The preparation of the food, as well as their meal companions, were carefully controlled to avoid impurity through nonobservance of the food rules or contact with people who were likely to be impure. The Pharisees believed that those who were consciously seeking God's way of living should be similarly observant. Hence, they were highly critical of Jesus' own meal practices.

Strict Sabbath observance was another key point. The Sabbath was to be kept holy, free from work. But what was "work"? This question was one of those that generated a plethora of case law or traditions. The regulations governing what constituted work on the Sabbath developed into a series of prescripts and prohibitions. This was another area of controversy with Jesus, whose Sabbath observance, they thought, was at best lax and at worst blasphemous.

According to Marcus Borg, tithing was a third major issue for the Pharisees that brought them into conflict with ordinary people. If people were properly observant Jews, they were effectively subject to double "taxation"—the Jewish tithe and Roman taxes. "Hence the Pharisees advocated an intensification of holiness precisely in the area in which the temptation to be non-observant was the greatest."[77] This does not feature prominently in their conflict with Jesus, however.

If strict Torah observance was the means of holiness, the Pharisees' primary understanding of holiness was separation. The holiness of God was centered in separation from all that defiles— if they were to be holy as God is holy, they, too, must be separate. As noted earlier, they believed this applied for *all* of Israel, not just the priests. Therefore, they were to be clean and pure—mainly by careful observance of purity and tithing regulations.

The problem of the land itself remained. It was to be holy as well because it was God's. But the land could only be pure when the Gentile occupying forces were no longer polluting it by their mere presence. Hence, the concern for holiness was the ideological or religious motivation for the Jewish resistance to the Roman occupation.[78]

Although some holiness groups separated from society, the

Pharisees advocated separation *within* society. The Pharisees maintained opposition to the ruling Temple elite, but they did not abandon the Temple as did the Qumran community. Increasingly they came to regard themselves as the alternative covenant community—the remnant.

Despite their efforts, the Pharisees knew that not all shared their intense commitment to purity. They acknowledged that such a state of purity did not exist in the land as a whole and among the people. They didn't disenfranchise their fellow Jews, however. They themselves lived according to that level of commitment and pointedly expected other holiness groups to do the same. According to Wright, in the face of social, political, and cultural pollution in society as a whole, they concentrated on personal purity and cleanness in such a way as to maintain an area of personal purity—an island of purity in a sea of pollution.

The primary motivation for the Pharisees was not political power. Their purity codes seem to be exclusively religious. Although they were "religious" in origin and intent, nevertheless it would be impossible to separate religion and politics. Their influence, then, was emphatically "political" in effect.[79] As Borg notes,

> Thus a confluence of currents combined to constitute the ideology of holiness. Yahweh was holy and Yahweh's people, living by an *imitation dei,* were to be holy. The land itself was holy and was to be kept pure. The Temple and Torah were both essential to holiness; the Temple was the center of holiness, and the holiness of the Temple, land, and people depended upon the careful observance of Torah. Moreover, the two major renewal movements were both committed to an intensification of holiness. Hence, in the quest for holiness, we find the religious dynamic which was the ideological cause of Jewish resistance to Rome.[80]

Jesus had His most sustained and serious clashes with the Pharisees. Some of these are reflected in the Gospels. But it is important to note that there was never any debate over whether holiness was essential: it was. The disagreements were over the means and the meaning of holiness.

The quest for holiness had a profound impact on all of second Temple Jewish society. Few groups in society, however, took the need for holiness to the extremes that our next group, the sectarian community at Qumran, did.

## 4. QUMRAN[81]

Qumran[82] is a particularly interesting part of the background to the Gospels, not least because of their use of the term "perfection." Qumran was clearly a holiness movement but unlike the Pharisees who saw themselves as being a holy remnant *within* society, Qumran saw itself as being the holy people *outside* society. In their view, separation from all possible contact with impurity was the only way to maintain the level of purity they thought essential to following God's Law. They even maintained a separate calendar from others in Judaism in order to maintain God's intention as they understood it from Scripture. They were, therefore, sectarian in outlook, probably closely linked to the Essenes. Significantly, they believed that a decisive turning point in history was arriving and that they were God's instruments for fulfilling His saving purposes.[83]

Scripture was central to their existence. It contained the mystery of God's purposes set down beforehand. Now God had made His hidden purposes known to them. They were, in fact, the people of the new covenant. Their community life was the fulfillment of prophecy, and Israel's story was now focused upon them alone. This sectarian perspective inevitably isolated them from society. So far as we can tell, they did not participate in the Jerusalem cult. As far as they were concerned, the Jerusalem Temple establishment was hopelessly corrupt, rendering the whole system ineffective. They may have seen themselves as "a kingdom of priests" performing the service of worship or atonement in place of the corrupt Jerusalem priesthood or perhaps even regarding themselves as the true temple. In either case, they saw themselves as the "spearhead of the divine purpose for the world" and therefore took themselves with utmost seriousness.[84]

In short, God's "eschatological salvation had already entered the present age in the history and experience of the community."[85]

Because Scripture was so central to their existence, they devoted themselves to the intense study of it and to rigorous application of the Torah. Their identity as the new people of God was articulated in the intensification of the rules of purity that were applied in the community.[86] They were the new covenant people, so the covenant law was kept. Although they were Jews by birth, they did not believe that made them automatically part of the new covenant community. Rather, they chose to leave the wider Jewish society and enter voluntarily into the community. They were accepted into it by the decision of existing members and then only on the basis of stringent qualifications that were followed during a probationary period.[87]

Obedience to the Torah not only implied a whole pattern of behavior but also applied to attitudes as well. Every law was to be observed with the whole heart. Thus they intended to live in complete conformity to the Law with outward performance matched by inward obedience. They believed that this level of perfection was possible now.[88] So conscious were they of this reality that they called themselves the "House of Perfection."[89] Their exalted claim did not exclude the need for progress in perfection, however. Nor were they blinded to the possibility of failure. They knew that a gap existed between the character of God, on the one hand, and the powers of evil working in and through humanity, on the other, resulting in a trait that Deasley calls the "human proclivity towards sin."[90] This human sinfulness was "resistant to any purification available in the present."[91] So they looked for a decisive work of the Spirit at the end of the days: "The Qumran expectation for the end-time was the abolition of innate sin and the recovery of the creation glory of Adam."[92]

The way of perfection was not an end in itself. It had a soteriological goal.[93] They were atoning for their own sins; they also saw themselves as in some sense atoning for the land and the people as a whole. Indeed, "the most striking of all their beliefs [was] . . . the conception of their duty as the making of expiation

. . . for the sins of the nation which had gone so far astray from the path of His will."[94] Because Israel had failed to keep the covenant and since the Temple worship was currently irredeemable, only the obedience offered by the community could save Israel. Their perfect obedience would be the fulfillment of Israel's covenant obligations. If they walked in the ways of perfection, they could offer to God the perfect worship He demanded, a worship that was in communion with the angels.[95] Nevertheless, they did not see themselves acting solely or independently of God. They were the agents of God's atonement through their offering of perfect obedience.[96]

A crucial aspect of Qumran theology was their emphasis upon the Spirit. Deasley comments: "The sect's emphasis on the spirit was a distinctive feature of its teaching; indeed, it is widely conceded that the Qumran community stands out as an exception in an era which confessed that, in general, the spirit was no longer at work. Not only did they believe that the spirit was actively at work in their community; they believed that through their community alone the spirit could be received."[97]

This corporate dimension of the work of the Spirit was critical to their existence. The Spirit was the agent of God's work in the community, so "exclusion from the community [was] exclusion from the spirit and exclusion from the spirit [was] exclusion from cleansing."[98] Only through the Spirit could the community walk in the way of perfection.

The Qumran practice of holiness might appear to have been a matter of external conformity to the Torah. But that would be a misreading of their perspective. For them, perfection had to be a combination of the internal and the external. "Rote-performance would not suffice. . . . ritual observance was valueless unless accompanied by the spirit of penitence. But equally since the law must be kept, they must not only be punctilious 'doers of the law,' but to guarantee this, the law must be tightened up to insure that no demand was overlooked."[99] Deasley's summary highlights this combination.

Perfection is an achievable state in the present in respect of compliance with sectarian law, a change of heart in regard to sin and God, and an anticipation of heaven itself by the assimilation of the worship of the earthly community into the worship of the holy ones who serve God face to face. This perfection is not merely desirable and attainable: it is indispensable if the sectarian community is to discharge its appointed function of atoning for the land. But it is also indispensable as the due fulfilment of the covenant obligation which the sectaries had freely undertaken: that is, of the responses of life and service which God requires. Therefore, perfection is both means and end—now.[100]

This meant that the task for the present was "observing the law with an emphasis on the need for inward obedience and submissiveness."[101] They maintained their insistence upon perfection in the present. "But its complete attainment in the present seems [only] to have taken place in worship where heaven and earth, present and future were fused in a unity as they discharged their most solemn obligation: offering atonement for sin."[102]

In sum, Qumran theology placed soteriology at the center of their belief. The performance of covenant obligations, which was the role of the community, had soteriology as its goal—the salvation of Israel. Qumran was under no illusions about the direness of the human condition. They lived with an eschatological tension between the demands of perfection and the inability to be perfect. Deasley concludes that "they lived at a point of soteriological tension for which they found no theological resolution within the present."[103]

Several significant features of Qumran theology emerge for our study. First, "perfection" was a widely used term referring to both outward obedience and inward direction of heart. Jesus' use of this language in Matthew has a clear second Temple context as well as an Old Testament background. Second, obedience could never be just outward conformity to the Law, but neither could it merely be inward assent without outward performance. Any critique of second Temple holiness movements that suggests they ignored the inner dimension of holy living is almost certainly wide of the mark. Third, they believed themselves to be in the last days and therefore they were God's new covenant people who would be embodying in itself the purposes of God for Israel. They were to be a holy people living holy lives in obedience to God's holy law so that they might be an atonement for the whole people of Israel. Their holiness had a redemptive goal beyond their own salvation, even if it meant separation from their fellows. Fourth, they believed perfection was possible now while simultaneously maintaining a keen awareness that there was a future dimension to this. Qumran hopes for the future were tied to a time when God would act, in concert with themselves, *"within* history to redeem his people and re-establish them *as* his people, within his holy Land and worshipping in a new Temple."[104] But this resolution was in the future. Finally, they were conscious of the Spirit's presence in their community. The view that God's Spirit was thought to be absent in late second Temple Jewish thought needs to be revised. Some groups may have taken that view, but it was not the view at Qumran nor the people of piety reflected in Luke 1 and 2.

## 5. Jesus and the Holiness Movements

This sketch of some of the beliefs and practices of other movements in Judaism has shown how widespread the concern for holiness was. The Pharisees and Qumran are prominent in the literature available to us. John the Baptist may also be treated as the leader of a reform movement within Judaism recalling the people of God to their intended purposes.

There are, of course, many similarities between the Jesus movement and others. They shared the same basic beliefs of all forms of Judaism. But more crucially, all the reform movements considered the condition of Israel to be dire and in need of rescue. The evidence was plain for them to see—the power of the Romans, the compromises made by the Temple authorities, the despair of the people. They all shared the desire for Israel to be rescued and to be what it should be. That made all of them "holiness" movements in some way or another. At several points, the beliefs of the Jesus movement, the Pharisees, and Qumran over-lap.

The eschatological tension observed in Qumran permeated other second Temple holiness movements as well. It is only re-solved in the Jesus movement. Jesus announced the arrival of the kingdom of God came in His person and work. That is not to say that the Jesus movement eliminated the future pole of the escha-tological tension. On the contrary, a collapse of the future into the present was never part of Jesus' teaching. But the emphasis upon the arrival of the Kingdom gave Jesus' teaching an edge. God's good purposes were being accomplished now in and through His ministry even if their consummation would be in the future.

There were also serious disagreements over key points of the holiness agenda. The implications of these disagreements were huge. Not least was fundamental disagreement over the connec-tion between holiness and ritual purity. This is the point at which Jesus' teaching shows its sharpest disagreement with most of the other holiness movements.

In an important study, Marcus Borg highlights Jesus' critique of the Pharisees implied by His table fellowship. Borg reminds us that meals were particularly highly regulated. In the later rab-binic texts that developed out of the Pharisaic movement of the late second Temple period, 229 of 341 regulations pertain to table fellowship. Pharisee piety centered around table fellow-ship. As Borg reminds us, "Disputes about table fellowship were not matters of genteel etiquette, but about the shape of the com-munity whose life truly manifested loyalty to Yahweh. Thus the meals of those belonging to the Pharisaic fellowships symbolized what was expected of the nation Israel: holiness, understood as separation."[105]

The importance of the meal as a marker of holiness helps to explain several Gospel conflict stories. In Mark 2:15-18,[106] for ex-ample, not only did Jesus call Levi, a tax collector, to follow Him but He went to dinner at Levi's house and is joined by "many tax collectors and sinners" (v. 15). The scribes of the Pharisees enter the story here and question His actions: "Why does he eat with tax collectors and sinners?" (v. 16). Jesus' response was that He was calling sinners, not the righteous (v. 17).

Behind this concern for table fellowship lay the issue of purity and holiness.[107] Sitting at table together was an expression of intimacy and fellowship that is quite foreign to the fast-food 21st century. By eating with tax collectors and sinners, Jesus was thought to be endangering His character as a holy person through contact with the contagion of sin. Not only were His dinner companions by definition impure, but the Pharisaic food rules were probably also ignored. Second, "for the Pharisees the meal had become a microcosm of Israel's intended historic structure as well as a model of Israel's destiny."[108] According to Borg, "Jesus' association with sinners and tax collectors appeared to threaten both the internal reform of Judaism and its solidarity over against the Gentiles. Moreover his table fellowship with outcasts challenged the understanding of God upon which the reform and solitary were based."[109] Jesus was thought to be polluting the holy people by breaking down the walls of separation.

Clearly, Jesus also thought that table fellowship was crucial. But His message was different. For Jesus, the meals were a prophetic representative act in which Jesus sets about restoring the marginalized to the people of God. He was gathering around Him a representative collection of those who had been placed on the fringes of society. The climactic prophetic representative act at the Last Supper with the representative figures of the people of Israel, the Twelve, was the anticipated re-creation of the new covenant community through Jesus' death and resurrection. In anticipation of the new people, in His meals He was bringing healing to the broken people of God and re-creating the true people of God. For Jesus, the mission was to *all* of Israel—and no one should be excluded. In fact, His message was precisely to those who were excluded from the holy people of God. In this new community God was re-creating an inclusive new people. The objections raised by Jesus' opponents were centered on what Wright calls "the scandalous implied re-definition of the Kingdom itself."[110]

Closely connected to this was the ritual washing of hands (see Mark 7). Hand washing was probably linked with priestly requirements. For the Pharisees, essentially a lay movement, this was an intensification of holiness by extending priestly purity to nonpriestly followers in the entire land. Jesus shared the notion of intensification of holiness but thought of it as an inner matter. He contravened an extension of priestly regulation to ordinary life thereby directly opposing the Pharisees. He called into question the way holiness could be achieved: "The equation between holiness and separation was denied."[111] For Jesus, defilement was a matter of the heart, not primarily a matter of performance.[112]

On the critical matter of Sabbath observance, Jesus reinterpreted the Torah. For Jesus, compassion trumped strict observance. In fact, Sabbath was a particularly good day to work compassion in Israel since the Sabbath was made for Israel, that is, for human beings.[113] Compassion was God's work. Thus, the sanctity of the Sabbath—its holiness—was best demonstrated by doing the merciful work of God. This penetrated to the inner meaning of Sabbath.

Jesus' understanding of holiness, then, involved a radical redefinition. Borg thinks of it as an alternative paradigm. Jesus, according to Borg, called into question the whole holiness-equals-separation motif. Instead, He focused upon a different aspect of God's holiness, His compassion, and that made a huge difference. The essence of holiness, then, was not separation but compassion, and this was the way in which God's people were to be imitators of Him—how they were to be His holy people. Borg notes, however, that this did not

> point to an absolute difference between Jesus and his opponents. For first-century Judaism the claim that God was holy involved no denial that God was compassionate, loving, etc., though it did circumscribe the sphere within which people were to imitate the compassion and love of God. Similarly, for Jesus the claim that God was compassionate involved no denial that God was also holy.[114]

Although Borg may draw an overly sharp distinction between

holiness and compassion, the key point to note was that in Jesus' view holiness did not require protection and insulation from sources of defilement. Holiness was contagious and a transforming power, not a power that needed protection. It was "an active force which overcame uncleanness. The people of God had no need to worry about God's holiness being contaminated. In any confrontation it would triumph."[115]

## 6. THE EARLY CHURCH CONTEXT

If the context in which we must understand Jesus is second Temple Judaism, it is equally clear that the theology of the Gospels must be understood in the context of the Early Church. We cannot go into great detail here except to observe two critical points.

First, the specific Christian interpretation of Scripture and God's good purposes expressed in the life of Jesus arose out of the appearances of the risen Lord and the presence of the Spirit in the Early Church. In this light, Jesus was confirmed as the climax of Israel's story and the locus of God's good purposes. *Christian theology emerged out of the experience of the new covenant community interpreted according to the Scriptures.* Theological development in the Early Church moved in precisely this direction—from experience to theology—and not the other way round.[116] According to Luke, the process of retelling the story of Israel in a new light was inaugurated by Jesus himself (see Luke 24:44-49). The continuation of the process of retelling and advancing the mission may be attributed to the empowering presence of the Spirit in their midst.

Second, the expansion of the Church beyond the bounds of Judaism, which began almost immediately, had to be explained as well.[117] This, too, was understood as part of the ultimate good purposes of the creator God, although it required a genuine conversion experience of the apostle Peter for this to be accepted (see Acts 10:1—11:18). Here again, the Spirit's activity in the advance of the gospel beyond the bounds of Judaism was explicitly tied to Jesus and the Spirit (see Acts 1:8).

The message that God's good purposes have come to their focus in Christ and that He has called together disciples to be His holy people, the beginnings of the re-creation of a kingdom of priests and a holy nation, impels the mission of the Church into the world.

# 2

# HOLINESS, JESUS, AND THE SPIRIT
## THE GOSPEL OF LUKE

In his excellent popular little book *We Need Saints,* Lieutenant Colonel Chick Yuill writes, "All too often our holiness teaching starts from the wrong place. Let us be clear that holiness does not begin at the point of surrender and crisis in the life of the believer. . . . [T]his is not the place to begin. It is too man-centred, too self-oriented, too sin-concerned. *The place to begin is with Jesus Christ and his perfect adequacy.*"[118]

Western Christianity has tended to focus upon the Cross to describe this adequacy. But the New Testament picture is at once deeper and broader. The full humanity of Christ is just as central to our salvation as His divinity. All of the Gospels are important for understanding the Incarnation. But the Gospel of Luke is particularly helpful because of the way in which it describes the birth, life, death, and resurrection of Jesus.

If we are indeed called to be God's holy people, how can we live holy lives today? The biblical answer is "through the ongoing presence of the Spirit." In some senses, Acts is full of examples of just how this worked out in the Early Church. The apostles in Acts, then, become the paradigm for our lives. We all want to add our own chapter to Acts in imitation of the apostles. Indeed, Paul tells his Corinthian readers to "be imitators of me, as I am of Christ" (1 Cor. 11:1).

But Luke actually offers a more nuanced paradigm. Jesus is the prime example of the work of the Spirit in a human being. Luke describes the work of the Spirit in Acts in terms that mirror the work of the Spirit in the life and ministry of Jesus as shown in the Gospel. The difference between the work of the Spirit in the Gospel of Luke and the Acts of the Apostles is primarily the *extent* of the Spirit's distribution ("all flesh") rather than the *character* of His work. This remains the same. Thus, in order to understand how we as Christians live our lives in the Spirit, we need to examine the relationship between Jesus of Nazareth and the Spirit.

## 1. THE BIRTH NARRATIVES

The birth narratives of Luke's Gospel put us immediately into the world of second Temple Judaism. Here we meet people of holiness, observant, pious Jews, longing for the consolation of Israel. Zechariah and Elizabeth "were righteous before God, living blamelessly according to all the commandments and regulations of the Lord" (1:6). Simeon is "righteous and devout, looking forward to the consolation of Israel, and the Holy Spirit rested on him" (2:25). Anna "never left the temple but worshiped there with fasting and prayer night and day" (v. 37). Indeed, Anna was called "a prophet" (v. 36), a woman attached to the Temple for decades.[119] Here we see instances of the Spirit working through "invasive prophetic speech."[120] The whole section demonstrates "the continuation of faithfulness to the Scriptures and guidance of the Spirit in God's one salvific purpose."[121]

As we have seen, Jewish piety is centered in the Temple because the Temple is the locus of God's dwelling place among His people.[122] The story begins in the Temple with the annunciation to the righteous priest, Zechariah, of the birth of John; the birth narratives close with Jesus in the Temple debating with the scholars and drawing attention to the Temple as His Father's house (2:50). Jesus' parents were also observant Jews (vv. 22-24, 39), with their religious lives centered around the great festival of Passover celebrated in Jerusalem (v. 41). Indeed, as far as the Lucan Jesus is concerned, God's new thing *could* have been centered in the Temple and Jerusalem (19:41-44; see also 24:52-53; Acts 1:4-5).[123] Something new is indeed afoot as seen from the frequent angelic interventions, and Israel could have been the center of it.

Luke's birth narratives are replete with references to the Spirit. This is in keeping with the Old Testament where the Spirit is active in specific events and came upon particular people at key points in the narrative. It is also a clear signal of God's gracious and continuing activity in the story of Israel. Despite the sense that Israel is still in exile, the references to the Spirit and the piety of the main characters in the drama demonstrate that God is still present and at work among His people. Crucially, the Spirit is active in the births of John and of Jesus.[124] John, we are told, is "filled with the Holy Spirit" even before he is born. Indeed, his mother, Elizabeth, is also "filled with the Holy Spirit" and prophesied.[125] For Luke, John is the last and greatest of the Old Testament prophets (7:24-28), the one with a special role and significance as the precursor to Jesus. But he is filled with the Spirit in Old Testament terms: "with the spirit and power of Elijah he will go before him . . . to make ready a people prepared for the Lord" (Luke 1:17). Clearly, he is a specific individual to whom the Spirit is given for a special purpose.

At the same time, it is clear that the presence of the Spirit is an indication of God's gracious interaction with the human story. Although John's conception is miraculous, it is the consequence of normal sexual intercourse. By contrast, Jesus' conception is without human initiative (vv. 34-35).[126] Here, allusions[127] to the creation stories may well be present. According to Gen. 1:2, the creative Spirit of God is brooding or hovering over the chaos. According to verse 28, humankind is created as a social being in the image of God.[128] Together these echoes suggest that the virginal conception of Jesus is understood by Luke to be a new creation, a new beginning for humanity. He is born through the "miraculous power of new creation"[129] as the first of the new humanity, the second Adam.

It might be objected that "second Adam" language is an unwarranted importation of Pauline language into Luke were it not for Luke's genealogy of Jesus, which ends with "son of Adam, son of God" (3:38). He seems to emphasize two points. First, Jesus' human origin is entirely due to God's gracious activity.[130] Here is the gracious God entering into human existence with a purpose, not just for the people of Israel but for all children of

Adam. Second, Jesus comes directly from God. As Richard Bauckham puts it, "Jesus' origin is unparalleled in previous human history since Adam and Eve. But God's direct creation of Adam and Eve *is* a kind of parallel. . . . Jesus is . . . a generation that comes directly from God as the very first did."[131]

But Jesus' origin is also unlike that of Adam and Eve. Jesus has a mother—a young, obedient woman who is a child of Adam and Eve. He is born of a woman—the birth story of all humanity. Neither the genealogy nor the virginal conception demand that Jesus be born through "immaculate conception" or of anything other than flesh of our flesh and bone of our bone. Jesus enters fully into our human condition through His birth, taking on our fallen flesh.[132]

Jesus, then, is a thoroughly human figure, the agent of God (see Luke 11:20, "the finger of God"). As Nolland observes, "Jesus takes his place in the human family and thus in its (since Adam's disobedience) flawed sonship; however, in his own person, in virtue of his unique origin (1:35) but also as worked out in his active obedience (4:1-13), he marks a new beginning to sonship and sets it on an entirely new footing."[133]

Jesus, of course, is also the Holy One, the Son of God. Two dimensions of this phrase are important. First, "Son of God" in second Temple Judaism did not have the full Chalcedonian ontological significance that the term has come to have.[134] Rather, the language of the annunciation to Mary (1:32-33) combines the Davidic messianic hope,[135] based on 2 Sam. 7:14,[136] with hope for justice, righteousness, and the restoration of Israel (see Isa. 11:1-4; 32:15; and Exod. 40:35). Son of God connotes "the special relationship of a person with God and that person's obedience to and representation of God on earth."[137] Jesus is thus the "fountainhead of Israel's restoration"[138] embodying in himself the hopes and aspirations for national restoration. It is precisely this hope that is so poignantly expressed through the Spirit-filled persons who, in the Magnificat, the *Benedictus,* and the *Nunc Dimittis* announce God's good purposes as social transformation and reconciliation.[139]

Second, He is also the unique Son of God. This works in two directions. On the one hand, Jesus sees himself representing the true Israel to God and before the people. On the other, He is acting for and as Israel's God for the people in a way that only God could do and be. Thus, although "Luke is not working with Johannine or later trinitarian categories, he is nonetheless moving towards a more ontological (and not only functional) understanding of Jesus' sonship. . . . [It] extends backwards to the prevenient work of God in his creation as a human being."[140]

This ontological[141] understanding of Jesus' unique Sonship often presents a problem to those who, in the final analysis, think that this identity excludes Jesus from actually being a pattern for humankind. In simplest terms, some think that Jesus' humanity is so different from ours that His life experiences must be completely irrelevant to us. It is important, however, to see how Luke understands that divinity. Luke pictures Jesus as having an unself-conscious and developing relationship with His Father (see 2:52). He enters human existence and is like us in every respect in that He starts life and continues it in the same conditions in which we live. He lives as a child, experiences hormonal changes and becomes a young adult male.

His conception, of course, is only the beginning. To use theological language for a moment, He sanctifies our humanity by taking on our flesh and through His life of obedience, His ministry, His death, resurrection, and ascension, at every point sanctifies our humanity. It follows, then, that Luke would agree with Paul's view that equality with God is not a matter of grasping but of giving (see Phil. 2:5-11), and that Jesus enters humanity on our side of the divine/human line, laying aside all of His prerogatives in order to be just like us but without sin (see Matt. 26:53).

## 2. JOHN AND JESUS

John the Baptist's preaching about Jesus in Luke 3:16 stated that, "He will baptize you with the Holy Spirit and fire." On the lips of the Baptist, this statement draws attention to the judging, purifying, and refining role he expects would be exercised by Jesus through the Spirit.[142] Both the Spirit and fire are seen as the means of purification in the culmination of God's good purposes now being experienced in the coming of the kingdom of God.[143] John seems to emphasize the judging aspect, which is the best explanation for why he sends his disciples to ask Jesus if He really is "the Coming One" or ought he to look for another one who, presumably, would be more active in judgment (7:18-23).

Luke almost certainly has more in view. He links this saying to Pentecost when he has the resurrected Jesus interpret the Baptist's saying in terms of the outpouring of the Spirit (Acts 1:4-5; 2:1-21). Although purification of hearts is not noted directly in Acts 2, Peter's sermon elicited a response to the Good News. His advice to those who responded is that they ought to repent, be baptized in the name of Jesus for the forgiveness of their sins and they would receive the Holy Spirit. Peter's later explanation of Pentecost at the Jerusalem Council draws explicit attention to the fact that God made no distinction between the Jews and the Gentiles by "giving them the Holy Spirit, just as he did to us; and in cleansing their hearts by faith" (15:8-9).

In these passages, Luke highlights the Christological center of Pentecost. Jesus, who is conceived by the Spirit and upon whom the Spirit descends, is not only the bearer but also the dispenser of the Holy Spirit. This is a rather important corrective to those who would have a Spirit-centered as distinct from a Trinitarian understanding of Christian holiness. It is the risen Christ who, having "received from the Father the promise of the Holy Spirit" (2:33), pours out the Spirit (see v. 17). Pentecost is a Trinitarian celebration in the Christian calendar.

## 3. Jesus' Baptism and Temptation

The next intersections of Jesus and the Spirit occur after His baptism and in the following temptation. Two interesting points are to be noted about the baptism narrative, both different from the Matthean version (Matt. 3:13-17). First, Luke does not emphasize either the work of John or the baptism of Jesus. According to Luke, John has already been imprisoned before the baptism story is even told (Luke 3:19-20). The baptism itself has been "stripped of all its details, is subordinated, linked to the baptism of all the people, and set in the past."[144] Matthew, by contrast, explains why Jesus would undergo a baptism for repentance (Matt. 3:14-15) and indicates that the descent of the Spirit occurred as Jesus came up from the water. Second, according to Luke, the Spirit descended upon Jesus while He was praying, some time after the baptism. Luke's focus is clearly upon Jesus and the Spirit.

All four Gospels agree that the Spirit came upon Jesus at the inauguration of His ministry. But Luke has a further emphasis: the descent of the Spirit upon Jesus is set in the context of prayer. Both aspects are significant. Before Jesus embarks upon His ministry, He is empowered by the Spirit sent from the Father. The One conceived by the Spirit and the One who has already been about His Father's business is the One on whom the Spirit descends. This descent of the Spirit, then, seems clearly linked to the mission God has given Jesus. In addition, by having Jesus at prayer, Luke teaches his readers about Jesus' relationship with this Father and His consciousness of the need for strength to carry out the mission God has given to Him. It is not by accident that Luke in Acts depicts the apostles at prayer on Pentecost and at other nodal points in their mission.

The Old Testament background provides important clues to the remainder of the narrative. Isa. 42:1, Ps. 2:7, and Gen. 22:2 all play a part.[145] According to Isa. 42:1, God will anoint His Servant with His Spirit and the Servant will bring about righteousness and justice.[146] The Servant will be God's agent of redemption and peace with justice. When combined with language borrowed from Ps. 2:7 and echoing Gen. 22:2, the voice from heaven confirms not only the scope of Jesus' mission but His identity as the beloved Son who sits on David's throne. Here we have the "unimpeachable sanction of Jesus with regard to his identity and mission."[147] Clearly, Luke does not take the view that this is Jesus' first experience of the Spirit. The point is rather that Jesus is about to undertake His servant-mission as laid upon Him by God. In communion with God, He receives the Spirit as the essential empowering for this ministry (see 3:22-23).

The first episode in Jesus' ministry is facing temptation (4:1-13). Echoes again resound from the Old Testament testing of Adam and Eve. Jesus, the representative Son of Adam who is also Son of God (3:38), empowered and equipped by the Spirit for His mission as the agent of God's good purposes, has all of this put to the test. Unlike his success with the first Adam, however, the tempter is unable to deflect Jesus from His God-ordained mission. To put it another way, "as man, he begins the restoration of creation's teleology by offering to the Father a true human obedience."[148]

The temptation stories in Matthew and Luke are very similar. But, again, Luke makes significant alterations. First, he links the temptation directly with the genealogy by placing the genealogy in an unexpected place. This surprises us.[149] Matthew has the genealogy at the beginning of his Gospel. Luke, however, ties the whole birth narrative and the identification of Jesus to the temptation narrative. Through the narrative sequence, Luke shows that Jesus enters into the test as "son of Adam, son of God." In short, He faces the temptations from the devil with a genealogy that parallels that of all other sons and daughters of Adam.

Second, Luke adds that Jesus returned from the Jordan "full of the Holy Spirit." At that point, He is "led by the Spirit in the wilderness" (4:1) where He is tempted by the devil for 40 days. Now His very identity and willingness to be obedient to the Father is put to the test. "This is Luke's narratological declaration that Jesus is not acting on His own. Empowered by the Spirit, Jesus is full of the Spirit, and inspired by the Spirit. His central, active role is therefore fundamentally as God's agent, and it is this special relationship and its implications that lie at the root of Jesus' identity in Luke-Acts."[150]

The key point for us is this: Jesus faces the test as a fully human being and He does so "full of the Holy Spirit" (v. 1). Then He returns "to Galilee in the power of the Spirit" (v. 14, NIV). It cannot be by accident that Luke describes Peter's confrontation with the authorities as "filled with the Holy Spirit" (Acts 4:8) and that all of those threatened with persecution are "filled with the Holy Spirit" (v. 31; see 7:55).

The implications of this point are enormous, of course. All too often our picture of Jesus is of a person, not quite like us, who, because He is the Son of God, succeeds in His perfect obedience to His Father. "Of course he is able to resist temptation," we say, "He's God, isn't He?" Indeed, a superficial reading of Jesus' response to the devil in Luke 4:12, "Do not put the Lord your God to the test," might be taken to mean that Jesus is seeing the devil off by asserting His divinity. But that would be to misread the text and the thrust of the whole narrative. These temptations are real. And Jesus faces these temptations as a human being, meeting their force in the power of the Spirit. In other words, He meets and defeats the tempter as a human full of the Holy Spirit, exactly as His followers are to meet temptation. As Graham McFarlane notes, "Without the Spirit's role, there is no meaningful and assuring doctrine of salvation. . . . this entails the assurance of what [Irving] calls 'holiness in the flesh'—an assurance that what God requires of us is possible due to the fact that it has been achieved by the Saviour under the same conditions as those in which every human being exists."[151]

One final point on the temptation narratives. Whatever view one has of the language and imagery of the New Testament, here we encounter directly the scope of the opposition to God's good purposes and the depth of the redemptive task facing Jesus.[152] The story reminds us again that God's mission, and ours, has cosmic significance and cosmic opposition even if it is played out in the mundane setting of natural desires, self-preservation, and the easy option.

## 4. THE SERMON AT NAZARETH

Jesus set His agenda for ministry (and for the mission of the Church) in the inaugural sermon at Nazareth (4:14-30). Lest any impression be given that the Spirit's presence in the disciple's life is confined to an inner, spiritual battle, Luke deliberately highlights Jesus' clear consciousness of the Spirit's anointing for His mission. Green tells us that there is an "inexorable relation of the Spirit's anointing and the statement of primary mission, 'to preach good news to the poor.'"[153]

The immediate context, of course, is clear. Jesus has already returned to Galilee "filled with the power of the Spirit"—note the parallel language in 4:1—and has already entered into His ministry. Now He sets out the manifesto of His ministry at Nazareth. The citation of Isa. 61, with its prophecy of the coming of the messianic herald and bearer of the Spirit, adds to this link between Jesus and the Spirit and gives an intensely Christ-centered focus on the Spirit. Jesus is following God's agenda as set out in the Scriptures. He has been anointed by the Spirit and is full of the Spirit for His mission. He has already demonstrated that He is the obedient Son of God ready, in the power of the Spirit, for the task that is facing Him. Jesus is, therefore, both the bearer of the Holy Spirit and acts in the power of the Spirit.

The subsequent narrative enables Luke to show what the positive implications of the Spirit's presence on Jesus are. But closer attention to the link between the sermon and the preceding temptation narrative may also show what the presence of the Spirit does *not* mean for Luke. In the narrative, Jesus has just returned from the wilderness where, full of the Holy Spirit and led by the Spirit, He has met and defeated the tempter as a human full of the Holy Spirit. In light of this story, the clause "the Spirit of the Lord is upon me" (4:18) takes on deeper significance.

All three temptations are related to the mission on which Jesus is about to embark. All three have a personal significance as well. Jesus' first temptation is to use His Spirit empowerment for His own interests—to satisfy His own needs for the legitimate things of life. In this case it is food. But the legitimate things of life are not the ultimate things of life. To fulfill a legitimate desire through the power of the Spirit at the tempter's behest would take Jesus' focus away from the word of the Lord. Jesus rejects any self-centered use of spiritual power, a lesson learned by Simon Magus in Acts 8:9-24. He is then tempted more directly to find an easier way to fulfill the task laid on Him by God, one that would not involve suffering and death. But that, too, is rejected because it means turning His back on God's path of costly service. Jesus knows that the beloved Son cannot fulfill the Father's purposes by ceding authority to the devil. Finally He is tempted to use the Spirit's power to draw attention to himself through a miraculous spectacle. But a spiritual spectacle with Jesus as the star is rejected as well. His role is the Suffering Servant, not the spectacular superstar. All three of these temptations are directed to a selfish use of the Spirit's presence.

A word must be stated about "good news to the poor." The term "poor" denotes people who are the marginalized of society, whether for economic or other reasons of dishonor.[154] Instead of being outside the boundaries of God's purposes, the marginalized are the objects of divine grace. Critical to this is the term "release," used twice here. "Release" is conventionally linked to forgiveness from sin. It is also linked to exorcism and healing, signifying that "healing is not only physical but also signifies wholeness, freedom from both diabolic and social restrictions"[155] as well as release from debts. The Jubilee motif is clearly significant here,[156] pointing to Jesus' belief that the day of God's eschatological salvation has dawned.

At the end of the sermon, the people are astonished at the "words of grace" that come from Jesus—a literary reference to the fact that Jesus is acting in the power of the Spirit of God. The subsequent narrative shows exactly how Jesus fulfills His mission. And when Jesus continues to remind them that God has always been interested, not only in the marginalized of Jewish society, but in all people, doubts turn to rejection. Jesus is announcing a mission to the impure and hated Gentiles as well, and that enrages His first hearers, according to Luke. So they reject Jesus, His mission, and His message. They would rather continue to be God's holy people their own way—keeping pure from contamination, defending God's holiness against the foreigners, the tax collectors, prostitutes, and sinners, keeping their theological categories clear.

## 5. REDEFINING HOLINESS

A major component of Jesus' confrontation with the Pharisees is over the definition of holiness. For the Pharisees, the essence of holiness is separation from anything and anyone that would render one impure. But the Lucan Jesus takes a different tack. In the stories and teaching between 4:31 and 7:23, Luke shows how Jesus lives His life of perfect obedience to the Father through the power of the Spirit. This is how one acts if the Spirit of the Lord is upon him or her. The events show that this is neither a self-centered piety nor cling-film wrapped purity. Jesus, the One on whom the Spirit dwells, demonstrates His understanding of the holy life by deed and word. Within this sequence, three aspects of Jesus' activity emerge, all of which transgress Pharisaic purity boundaries.

The sequence begins with Jesus as exorcist. When confronted in the synagogue by a man with an unclean spirit, Jesus, named the Holy One of God by the unclean spirit, is triumphant and casts out the unclean spirit (4:33-34). The confrontation with the forces of evil, who have already been engaged in the temptation narrative, continues. Jesus puts His own purity at risk in this and the other situations narrated in this sequence. Equally as interesting is the frequent reference to touch, since impurity could be contracted by touch. Jesus deliberately touches the unclean (v. 40), the lepers (5:13), the disabled (6:8), and the bier of a dead person (7:14). He heals the servant of a Gentile centurion. Each one of these actions exposes Jesus to impurity. But in each instance, the holiness of Jesus conveyed through His touch is stronger than the impurity conveyed in the contact. According to 6:19, the power of Jesus' healing is transmitted in some way by touch. Instead of Jesus acquiring impurity, the unclean spirit is exorcised, the isolated and impure leper is cleansed, the sick are healed, and the dead boy is raised.

His table fellowship is also open to question. In 5:29 He is shown at table with many tax collectors and sinners. This presented particular problems to the Pharisees, who kept their community pure through rigorous application of priestly food rules. If

Jesus were announcing God's rule, why is He associating with those who are not leading holy lives? The Pharisees could not understand why Jesus persists in entering into intimate fellowship with sinners by actually eating with them.

In the midst of this activity comes the sermon on the plain (6:20-49). Among its important features is the fact that Jesus pronounces blessing upon the marginalized and the dispossessed while warning those who are comfortable now. By His actions and His teaching, Jesus is demonstrating the implications of the Spirit's anointing and fulfilling His own announcement of the Good News.

But not all understand. Even John the Baptist has questions. At the end of this sequence, John sends two of his disciples (7:18-23) to inquire of Jesus about the nature of His mission. Jesus' response is instructive. The coming one is to do precisely what Jesus has been doing. In fact, the narrator in verse 21 deliberately makes the point that "Jesus had just then cured many people of diseases, plagues, and evil spirits, and had given sight to many who were blind" (v. 21). With that in mind, Jesus responds: "Go and tell John what you have seen and heard: the blind receive their sight, the lame walk, the lepers are cleansed, the deaf hear, the dead are raised, the poor have good news brought to them. And blessed is anyone who takes no offense at me" (vv. 22-23). Time and again the compassion of Jesus for those who are the marginalized overrides the legitimate concern for purity. Jesus is on God's mission. Jesus' apparently cavalier attitude to the purity rules means opposition is strong and, furthermore, has a scriptural basis.

For Jesus, the problem is that His opponents seem to miss the central point about God's holiness. God is not a finger-wagging, fussy, and stern patriarch who watches vigilantly lest someone break a rule. Rather, His holiness is His essential character, shown as a gracious and loving God, slow to anger and plenteous in mercy. So Jesus tries to adjust their thinking about God. He does so partly through the parables.

Jesus' parables in Luke do not say much about holiness in any direct fashion. But they do tell us a great deal about what God is like. And when we catch a better glimpse of God, we can better understand the command to be holy. The group of three parables in Luke 15 is particularly illuminating.[157] All presuppose the same narrative setting. In the background are tax collectors and other outcasts; in the audience are the Pharisees and scribes (vv. 1-2).

The story of the lost sheep is remarkable because of its audacity. This shepherd is not wise by normal standards. Instead of saying to himself, "I must cut my losses and protect the 99 sheep that I still have," he risks all to search for the lost one. He leaves the rest of the flock in the wilderness, of all places. And he doesn't give up until he has rescued this one sheep. When he does find it, he carries it home and invites all his neighbors to a party simply because he has found a lost sheep.

What is the point of the story? Sometimes we have sought the point by analyzing sheep—sheep are wanderers. This sheep leaves the security of the flock and wanders away bit by bit. Nothing sinister in its drifting away—merely prone to wander. But that is not the point made by Jesus. Even if the sheep does not really "repent," Jesus is quite explicit: God is the persistent, seeking, gracious, and loving God who extravagantly celebrates the rescue of every single repentant sinner.

The next story is of the lost coin. Here the main character is a poor woman. Some think this parable centers on a special coin, perhaps lost through carelessness. On this reading, the message then becomes one of prudence. But again, that is not the point made by Jesus. Again He is quite explicit: the point of the story is celebration over the rescue of one person. The rescue of each individual is important. The joy in heaven over one sinner who repents seems to be out of all proportion even if in this case 1 coin out of 10 represents a greater percentage than the rescue of 1 lost sheep out of 100. Interestingly, both stories tell of a celebration the cost of which could well exceed the value of the recovered sheep or coin.

The third story of the lost son centers on a younger brother who leaves his father's home quite deliberately, demands his in-heritage, emigrates to a far country—Gentile territory—wastes the whole of his inheritance in debauchery, and becomes a swineherd, even eating with the pigs. One can hardly imagine a lifestyle more abhorrent to Jewish sensitivities. His impurity knows no bounds. His father considers him to be dead. In desperation the lost son decides to return to his father's home and beg forgiveness. His expectations are as low as his self-esteem.

When the prodigal begins his journey home, the parable takes a quite unexpected turn. In a patriarchal society, fathers are figures of dignity and authority. This father is different. When this father sees his bedraggled son in the distance, his immediate response is compassion. This father sets aside all dignity, runs toward his son, embraces and kisses him. This public display of reconciliation with the son who has humiliated him, even before the son asks for forgiveness, is astonishing. The son does seek forgiveness, but his father cuts short the prodigal's prepared speech. For the father, the only important thing is that his son has returned. Celebration is the order of the day, not a recounting of the past. The only thing that matters is the fact that "this son of mine was dead and is alive again; he was lost and is found" (15:24). The robe, ring, and sandals together with the public celebration all point to the complete restoration of the son.

Meanwhile, his elder brother has been the model citizen. He has served his father faithfully, working on the estate, not once being disobedient, following the rules to the letter. But the elder brother is as tragic in his own way as is his younger brother. And the contrast with the father could hardly be greater. The elder son is in the field, rather than on the lookout for his brother; he keeps his distance from the music and dancing; when he hears of his brother's return, he is angry rather than compassionate; he refuses to enter into the family celebration, remaining aloof from the rejoicing; he is judgmental rather than forgiving. But this father loves his elder son with the same unquenchable love, and so goes out to find him. Celebration of the restored relationship is essential, but that celebration should include the elder brother. The parable leaves the ultimate response of the elder brother open, but the graciousness of the father is unquestioned.

Against the background of 15:1-2, all three parables make the same points. First, Jesus is inviting the Pharisees to join Him in rejoicing that the sinners and the outcasts are, once again, part of the holy people of God. To be sure, these sinners have returned to God through a means not prescribed directly by the Torah, but return they have. Celebration of the return of the marginalized and welcome into the intimate fellowship of the community are central to God's holy people.

Second, Jesus tells us some important things about God. In the first parable, He is like the shepherd—the seeking God. In the second, He is like the poor woman—the searching God. In the final parable, He is like the wealthy landowner—the waiting father. All three point to the infinite and amazing grace of God.

Third, Christian holiness is not demonstrated by following a moral code. Legalism bedeviled the Pharisees. But holiness movements need not be legalistic. Jesus' holiness movement is different. For Jesus, holiness is "not a status to be possessed and hedged around for self-protection, but a relationship to be celebrated and shared."[158] We come again and again to the same point: holiness is centered in relationship to the Holy One, not performance of any holiness code. Furthermore, it is outward-looking and inclusive, not insular and exclusive.

Fourth, if God's grace and His mission become the center of Holiness living, Holiness people will still have "high moral standards." The reason, however, will be different. No longer will it be because they are living according to guidelines for holy living; no longer will they be judgmental moralists thundering against the evils of society. Rather, they will live lives honoring to God in grateful response to, and wholly dependent upon, grace and they will be channels of that grace even to the most abhorrent and detestable.

Grace is prior to Christian holiness. We are always in danger of getting the order wrong: repentance then forgiveness then acceptance seems to be our preferred order. But the order in these parables seems to be acceptance and forgiveness then repentance. The priority is on grace, not on performance. Holiness is founded upon the graciousness of God, not human ability to perform.

## 6. ASPECTS OF HOLINESS IN LUKE

According to Luke, therefore, Jesus is conceived by the power of the Spirit, commissioned by the Spirit, led by the Spirit, anointed by the Spirit, full of the Holy Spirit, and filled with the power of the Holy Spirit. His entire ministry is conducted in the Spirit.

Three crucial points emerge from this brief survey. First, the teaching has a *Trinitarian focus*. Jesus is in intimate relationship with the Father through the Spirit. This is what John characterizes as mutual indwelling, a point to be taken up in the next chapter. He is the Holy One, the Son of God. As such, He not only bears the Spirit but is the giver of the Spirit as well. He has no need for cleansing, nor has He ever been the disobedient son.

But can He be the real pattern for us? Does this not mean that Jesus' life, after all, only *seemed* to be like ours? To put it in its crudest terms, is Jesus merely "slumming it" with us for a time? Luke's answer to that question comes in his second crucial point: the *incarnational focus*. Jesus, the fully human person, takes on our fallen humanity and lives His human life from beginning to end in and through the Spirit. He enters fully into our human condition, assuming our brokenness, but without sin. He meets our real enemy, overcomes real temptation, carries out a genuine ministry, makes real decisions in our real world, all in the power of the Spirit. He lives His life in perfect obedience through the power of the Spirit. By paralleling Luke and Acts, Luke draws attention to the nature of the Christian life: born of the Spirit, sent out by the Spirit, led by the Spirit, filled with the Spirit, anointed by the Spirit, empowered by the Spirit, all in and through the name of Jesus.

Finally, Jesus announces good news to the poor, a message that leads to a radical redefinition of Christian holiness. No longer is holiness to be conceived of essentially as separation. Rather holiness is contagious, outgoing, embracing, and joyous.

It seeks the lost and rejoices when they are found because God's holy people are filled with the Spirit. Their lives mirror God's holy, seeking love for all His lost creation.

The great hymn of John Henry Newman, "Praise to the Holiest in the Height," captures something of the link between Jesus' life and death and our redemption:

### Praise to the Holiest in the Height
*Praise to the Holiest in the height,*
*And in the depth be praise;*
*In all His words most wonderful,*
*Most sure in all His ways.*

*O loving wisdom of our God!*
*When all was sin and shame,*
*A second Adam to the fight*
*And to the rescue came.*

*O wisest love!—that flesh and blood,*
*Which did in Adam fail,*
*Should strive afresh against the foe,*
*Should strive and should prevail.*

*And that a higher gift than grace*
*Should flesh and blood refine,*
*God's Presence and His very Self,*
*And Essence all divine.*

*O generous love! That He Who smote*
*In Man for man the foe,*
*The double agony in Man*
*For man should undergo.*

*And in the garden secretly,*
*And on the Cross on high,*
*Should teach His brethren, and inspire*
*To suffer and to die.*

*Praise to the Holiest in the height,*
  *And in the depth be praise;*
*In all His words most wonderful,*
  *Most sure in all His ways.*
    —John Henry Newman (1801-90)

# 3

# HOLINESS AND THE TRINITY
## THE GOSPEL OF JOHN

In the last chapter, we suggested that Luke tells the story of Jesus, Son of Adam, Son of God, who embarks upon the mission God has given Him as His[159] Agent, announcing and inaugurating God's new day for the people of Israel, and, therefore, for the entire world. In Jesus, God has made a new beginning for humanity. Jesus is the Second Adam who succeeds where the first Adam fails. He obediently undertakes the rescue mission to which God has called Him despite temptation to seek another direction.

All of this is done in and through the power of the Spirit by the One who is conceived by the Spirit, filled with the Spirit, empowered by the Spirit, and led by the Spirit. In all of this, Luke sees Jesus as a paradigm, a pattern for the Christian life of holiness, which is to be lived in and through the power of the Spirit. The God who calls us to holiness has shown us how to live as His holy people. It is not in our own strength but in and through the power of the Holy Spirit, lived in the context of the world, the flesh, and the devil, just as the Second Adam, Jesus, the Savior of the world, did. It is a life given over to God's mission, characterized by His compassion and His desire that all should be part of His great redemptive purposes. In the Acts of the Apostles, Luke gives further evidence of how the life of holiness is to be lived, again through the indwelling Holy Spirit in believers. Underlying this reading of Luke, we suggested, was an incipient Trinitarian model of God inextricably bound to an incarnation model of Jesus Christ that has Father, Son, and Spirit active in all dimensions of the life of the Incarnate One.

But if Luke points in the direction of the indwelling Holy Spirit, the Gospel of John takes the notion of indwelling on to an-

other plane altogether. Here the discussion on holiness takes another focus, again one that is understated, particularly in Western
Christianity. The question to be addressed all too briefly in this
chapter is this: "What relationship does the sanctification of believers have with mutual indwelling according to John 17?"

The language of John 17 immediately presents us with some
challenges. Although the writer makes no mention of the Holy
Spirit in this so-called high priestly prayer, we can just about understand the idea of the Spirit's presence in our lives. In that
sense, we can grasp the notion of God dwelling in us. After all,
we regularly hear the phrase "filled with the Holy Spirit" and
have been steeped in Paul's language of "in Christ." We can also
comprehend something of the intimacy between Father and Son
that greets us in John 17 because we are able, by analogy, to
imagine an intimacy of relationship between a parent and child.
The notion of a mutual indwelling of believers *in God,* however,
is almost beyond our comprehension. It sounds suspicious, almost pantheistic or new age. But that is precisely the kind of language that Jesus' prayer in John 17 uses. Here we have a note of
unique intimacy: Jesus looked up to heaven and said, "Father,
glorify me in your own presence with the glory I had in your
presence before the world existed" (v. 5). It is as if we were invited into the intimacy of a family conversation between Father and
Son, one that expresses both union and communion: between
Father and Son; between God and believers; and between believers. How shall we understand this language? And what are its
implications for Christians?

Even the most inattentive theology student cannot help but
observe the fact that the Jesus of the fourth Gospel speaks in a
quite different way from the synoptic Jesus. The late Bishop Robinson thought of the fourth Gospel as expressing Jesus' thoughts
from the inside, as it were.[160] But this prayer is a public one, precisely so disciples can note the nature of the relationship into
which they are invited to enter. Older commentators spoke of
this as a mystical union. This is true but not restricted to mystics!
Because it requires us to reflect on the relationship between Fa-

ther and Son as the model for the relationship between believers and God, and between believers, John 17 is a central holiness text. Instead of turning directly to John 17:17, however, I propose to build the case on rather different grounds.

# 1. THE MODEL FOR MUTUALITY: "THAT THEY MAY BE ONE, AS WE ARE ONE" (17:11)

## 1.1. God as Trinity

The complexity of this issue emerges right at the start in our thinking about God. When I was a theological student back in the last century, my dim recollection is that the "doctrine of God" started with the proofs for the existence of God from Aquinas through Kant to Schleiermacher. These were followed by a consideration of the attributes of God—omniscience, omnipresence, and omnipotence. As I recall, little attempt was made to anchor these doctrines in Scripture—it seemed more important to debate the philosophical dimensions of these abstractions. Not surprisingly, the God who emerged was more the God of the philosophers than the God of Abraham, Isaac, Jacob, and Jesus. Christology was the second topic, but we struggled to understand how Jesus could be fully human as well as fully God. It always seemed that Christ's divinity overwhelmed His humanity to such a degree that my views, like those of most grassroots evangelicals, were probably borderline docetic.[161] Any discussion of the doctrine of the Spirit was even more restricted—in fact, I cannot remember ever considering the Spirit apart from talking about "the baptism of the Spirit" and "the gift of tongues." As a consequence, we tended to think of God first as a singular being rather than thinking of God as Trinity.[162] All of this, I must stress, was due to my indolence as a student rather than any deficiency in the classes.

As for Trinity, the most that I could have said was that the doctrine of the Trinity was at best a mystery and at worst completely illogical. It was an arcane doctrine of the Church that we affirmed (not often, for the Creeds were rarely recited),[163] but was popularly thought to be in the category of "how many angels can dance upon the head of a pin." In many ways, my whole under-standing was stuck in a scholastic mold owing a great deal to Descartes (then one of my philosophical heroes) and the Enlight-enment. Contemporary theologians like Barth, Brunner, and Bult-mann were considered to be great neoorthodox thinkers, but I really only learned about their work through the eyes of Carl H. F. Henry and other conservative theologians of the day. En-gagement with Barth, as I recall, was restricted to his doctrine of revelation in Scripture and therefore whether his theology was "safe" for conservative evangelicals. Had we looked at Barth more closely, we would have seen that his whole *Church Dog-matics* "can be read as a thorough-going attempt to reassert the centrality of the doctrine of the Trinity by grounding it in the nar-rative of God's relationship with Israel and the Church, both of which have their ultimate center in Christ."[164]

Now, this is my memory, but years of teaching Christian un-dergraduates suggests to me that my thoughts are widely shared. Significant and very positive developments have taken place in the last two decades, however.[165] Most important has been a massive revival in the doctrine of the Trinity. These developments have taken place on three fronts.

First, theologians are now returning to the view that the *bibli-cal narratives* concerning God's interaction with the world are the proper starting point for any attempt to understand the Trinity rather than the abstractions of a Plato or a Plotinus. As noted in the introductory chapter, theology developed from the experience of the community of faith. Its movement from Judaism to the wider Gentile world inevitably led to a reformulation of biblical categories in widely divergent cultural and linguistic contexts, but the basis for Christian theology still needed to be the encounter with God to which the foundation documents, the Scriptures, bore witness. Scripture told of encounter with, and experience of, the one God as Yahweh, as the Incarnate Christ and as the ever-present Holy Spirit. As Colin Gunton puts it, "We know God be-cause and as the Father comes into free relation with us and with the world through his Son and Spirit. It was by drawing out the implications of that simple teaching that the early church came, over centuries of debate, to formulate the doctrine of the Trinity."[166] Here is the self-revelation of God as Trinity, which theologians have called the "economic" Trinity—an unfortunate choice of word for our culture because it conjures up images of God as Minister of Finance or Chancellor of the Exchequer,[167] but which simply refers to God in relation to the created order.

But God also has a history, or, to put it another way, the relation with the created order is merely a chapter in the story of God.[168] This is the story of the being of the Trinity in itself. Theologians sometimes speak of this as the "immanent" Trinity because it speaks of the internal being of God, the Three. Our knowledge of this, of course, also depends upon the revelation of God as experienced by the created order in relation to God.[169] That is not to say that we have a full picture of the Trinity in its essential being. But from our perspective, as Cunningham observes, "We cannot even separate out the categories of the 'immanent' and the 'economic' Trinity—let alone privilege one over the other."[170] From that experience we gain an inferential understanding of the Three. Once again, the biblical narratives are central in this revelation.

Second, modern Trinitarian theologians are very interested in the *practical implications* of Trinitarian theology. Here one can see the "earthing," as it were, of the great Trinitarian discussions concerning the eternal "processions" or, in a term that we might find more comprehensible, "missions," a debate into which I do not wish to enter and to which I could contribute nothing. Cunningham traces an interest in practical application primarily to the work of Jürgen Moltmann, but if this is so, it certainly has been important in the work of other theologians, such as Clark Pinnock.[171]

Third, recent Trinitarian theologians are all agreed on the central concept of *relationality* as the primary way of understanding the Trinity. Many scholars suggest that this emphasis may be traced to the renewed conversation between Western Christianity and Greek patristic thought. This has led to a greater awareness of the importance of the Trinity in Eastern Orthodoxy and a genuine dialogue with the Eastern Church.[172] It can also be traced to the reaction against the individualism of modern Western culture. Cunningham sees this as part of the postmodern rethinking of the concept of personhood in which "the Enlightenment idea of *person* as an isolated individual consciousness, theoretically detachable from the rest of the world, has been called into question. Personhood cannot be divorced from relation—a claim that seems to be substantiated in a wide variety of humanistic disciplines, from sociology and psychology to history and literature."[173] Even the language of our great hymn to the Trinity—"God in three persons, blessed Trinity"—is open to misunderstanding, the type of misunderstanding that prompts Cunningham to revert to Gregory of Nazianzus' "the Three" in order to avoid any semantic interference from the word "person" in the direction of individualism.[174]

But what does relationality mean in general terms? The key point is that God cannot be understood as an isolated singularity.[175] The Three "mutually constitute one another to such a degree that we cannot speak of them as 'individuals.'"[176] Just as the Three exist in dynamic interrelationship with one another so that one can never speak of the one without implying the Three, God must be thought of as a social being, a Being-in-Community,[177] existing only in the dynamic of a perpetual relationship of Holy Communion. Father, Son, and Spirit exist as divine entities in a social Trinity; that alone can account for what Pinnock calls the "sheer liveliness of God."[178] This relationship is one of *love* that Ware, in a very pregnant phrase, describes as "an unceasing movement of mutual love."[179] Pinnock comments, "As a circle of loving relationships, God is dynamically alive. There is only one God, but this one God is not solitary but a loving communion that is distinguished by overflowing life."[180] In sum, the Trinity in itself is "a community of love and mutuality."[181] This is the relationship to which Jesus refers in His prayer: "Father, I desire that those also, whom you have given me, may be with me where I am, to see my glory, which you have given me because you loved me before the foundation of the world" (John 17:24).

There are, of course, enormous implications that come from this. Trinity in loving communion is the basis of God's relationship with the created order and the origin of the perpetual *mission* of God to the created order. We see this relationship in the actions of the triune God who creates, redeems, and brings all things to their good purposes. But once we have seen His actions, we must not suppose that we have encompassed God in the Three. Although the actions may appear temporal, from God's perspective, "They are all wholly, equally and eternally constitutive of God's loving relationship with the world."[182] The external work of God in the created order is the expression of who God is in the Three.

If this is so, then the notions of *relationality, love,* and *mission,* based as they are upon who God is and how the Trinity works, are critical for aspects of Christian holiness in the fourth Gospel. Perhaps we can unpack them a little more as they may be seen in John 17. But first, at the invitation of John 1:1-4, we need to take a brief look at the creation story.

## 1.2. Trinity and Creation

The words of the Johannine Jesus in 17:1-5 clearly point to a relationship between Father and Son that predates human history. This is hardly surprising in light of the introduction to the fourth Gospel in 1:1-4. The language in these two passages certainly encourages theological reflection on the preexistence of the Son. But there are also implications for the notion of Trinity and its relations to creation. Although there is no explicitly Trinitarian language here, the words "before the world began" (17:5, NIV) suggest that it is possible to think about precreation in terms of the relationship of Father, Son (and, implicitly, Spirit). We turn, therefore, to the primal stories in Genesis to cast illumination on John 17.

When one looks at the creation stories in Genesis, it is clearly stretching the imagination to see "Trinity" written on every line—unless, of course, careful attention is given to the rest of the canon in an exercise in intertextuality.[183] When one comes to this text in light of the story of God as narrated in the rest of Scripture, some interesting possibilities emerge. First, Gen. 1:1-3 does not exclude a notion of Trinity; here we can see God as the source of all things, with the life-giving Spirit[184] brooding over the waters and God's word, which goes forth from Him in creative power. These are what Cunningham, following Augustine, calls *"vestigia Trinitatis:* triune marks."[185] When we turn to Gen. 1:27, the language is even more suggestive. Scholars have long noted that the name of God here is in a plural form (Elohim). This is frequently the case in Genesis,[186] but in this passage God speaks in the plural form as well. This has usually been explained as a plural of majesty or as a reference to the heavenly assembly.[187] However, as Cunningham observes, "This word can also be read as implying differentials within God."[188] This falls far short of Old Testament proof for the Trinity, of course, but a hint in this direction is not inconsistent with the interpretation of Gen. 1:1-3 just noted.

More important, however, is the statement that humankind was created in the image of God: "So God created humankind in his image, in the image of God he created them; male and female he created them" (Gen. 1:27). At first reading, this seems to indicate that God must be somehow related to gender. But to read the text this way is to reverse "image" and "source." We cannot read gender back into deity on the basis of this (or any other) text. The image of God is a plurality because God exists in plural form.

The implications are far-reaching. Humankind in its gender differentiation points to diversity within unity. As Gunton observes, "In this most central of all human relatedness is to be found a finite echo of the relatedness of Father, Son and Holy Spirit. . . . [T]o be in the image of God is to be called to a relatedness-in-otherness that echoes the eternal relatedness-in-otherness of Father, Son and Spirit."[189] On reflection, this is not at all surprising. If we are to think of God as a relationality, as I have been arguing, then it must follow that those created in His image would likewise exist in relationality. And this is precisely what we find confirmed in the second creation narrative. Here, God sees that it is not good for "Adam" to be alone. So from this solitary being, God forms two beings.[190]

Human beings, created in the image of God, were created

to be in relationship. We, too, are social beings, beings-in-community. There is more. According to the Genesis narratives, humanity was created as part of the whole created order and placed in the garden. The man comes from the same soil as do the beasts, yet he alone is a "living soul." The man was to exercise dominion over the created order, not in any tyrannical sense but as its representative. Taken from the same dust and existing in the image of God, humankind was to give voice on behalf of the entire created order to its Creator. Dominion was given "to enable the creation to praise its maker. . . . [T]o be in the image of God is therefore to be called to represent God to the creation and the creation to God."[191]

A key characteristic of the love relationship that is present in the Holy Trinity is that it has always been outward-looking. The very act of creation, epitomized by the creation of humans, points this way. A community of being was the intended shape of human creation existing in loving relationship. In creation, humanity was given the love-gift of freedom to choose to love. In this, humankind was also to represent God, to reflect God's image, a loving relational being in godly harmony with all others within the created order.

This story goes badly wrong. Love cannot be a matter of coercion. Love, the freely given gift from God, was turned inward by humankind. Humanity sought to evade its Creator and exercised love in a self-centered way. Into the idyllic garden came chaos. Each of the relationships in which humankind was created was disrupted in the Fall: God and His human creatures; male and female; humans and the entire created order. Instead of living as a social being mirroring the image of God in loving and constant fellowship with the Creator and in harmony with all of creation, both sentient and nonsentient, every one of these relationships was distorted. No longer was the relationship with God unclouded; and the relationship between men and women, the primary model of God's relationality, was fraught with pain, sorrow, and mistrust. Creation itself feared and distrusted humanity. No longer could humankind, created in the image of God, per-

form its intended function as the representative of the created order in the divine relationality. Instead, life became a struggle for
existence. The plight of humanity and the entire created order
was of chaos and spiraling despair. The marred image of God in
humanity now reflected an idolatrous image of God, mirroring
humanity's own idolatrous creations, instead of reflecting the
true image of the loving creator God.

These primal stories are the essential basis for understanding
the whole Gospel, not least in unpacking the meaning of Jesus'
prayer in John 17. In summary, let's pull together some of the
ideas that have emerged in our discussion. First, God is a triune,
social being of relationality. Any other understanding of God
leaves us with significant problems in understanding ourselves,
not to mention conceptualizing God. Second, the essence of this
relationality is a perpetual movement of love. The triune God
cannot be conceived of as static. Third, God's love is always outward-going rather than inward-looking. Indeed, any other understanding of love is a distortion. Fourth, creation itself is an expression of God's outward-looking love. God does not need the
created order in order to be God, but creation exists because of
the love of God. Fifth, humanity is created in God's image,
which means that humankind is also a social being. Therefore,
the God-designed destiny of humans is to be in relationship:
with the rest of the created order, with fellow human beings and
with the triune God. Sixth, humanity is to mirror the image of
God to the rest of creation and to respond to God on behalf of
creation. This combines the ideas of stewardship and priesthood.
Seventh, as a creature of creative love, humanity is given the
love gift of freedom to choose to love. Hence, the relationship of
the entire created order to the Creator is one of freedom, not coercion. Eighth, the Fall marred all relationships: God and His
creatures; male/female; humans/creation. No longer is humanity
able to represent God to the created order or to represent the
created order within the divine relationality. Western individualism is but one symbol of humanity's alienation from God and
within humanity itself. The most grotesque symbol of human

alienation is the domination system supported by personal, corporate, and state violence against our fellow humans and the rest of the created order.

## 2. Participation in Mutuality

### 2.1. Christian Unity: "That They May Be One, as We Are One" (17:11)

Perhaps more than any other section of Scripture, John 17 expresses the desire for Christian unity. Jesus prays that His disciples will be one. But Jesus is clear—the ground for Christian unity is not of human origin. Although our desire comes from the innate sense of needing to fulfill our purposes by modeling our Creator, we can no more create this unity ourselves than we can restore our relationship with God ourselves. The seeking and redeeming love of God brings us to the unity of Father, Son, and Spirit as a continuing and sustaining act of sheer grace.

As noted earlier, this prayer is a public prayer, a family conversation to which the disciples are allowed to listen (see especially 17:1-5). They hear of the love-quality of the Trinity[192] (17:24, 26: "because you loved me before the foundation of the world . . . so that the love with which you have loved me may be in them") and capture a glimpse of its intimacy. Jesus' disciples are to experience that kind of unity. On the historical level, it is clear that Jesus does not speak directly of the Spirit here, but John 17 has an immediate literary context, the Upper Room Discourse. In this concentration of teaching that Jesus has given to His disciples, the Spirit has been prominent. Jesus has promised, in 14:16-18, 20-21, that "I will ask the Father, and he will give you another Advocate, to be with you forever. . . . You know him, because he abides with you, and he will be in you. I will not leave you orphaned; I am coming to you. . . . On that day you will know that I am in my Father, and you in me, and I in you. They who have my commandments and keep them are those who love me; and those who love me will be loved by my Father, and I will love them and reveal myself to them." Jesus has already spoken of the way in which this mutuality will occur. It is through the Spirit, who will be with them and abide in them forever. A further aspect of this promise is also important. In this and the rest of the Upper Room Discourse, the Spirit is closely connected to the love in the community, the sign that they are Jesus' faithful disciples. Jesus' explicit command to them is this: "that you love one another as I have loved you" (15:12). But if the Spirit is indeed the "oneness of the love of Father and Son, Spirit is the source of the oneness of believers in the fellowship of love, creating relationships and bringing about a common life."[193]

Several summary points need to be noted. First, this unity cannot be conjured up through any concerted attempt by ecclesiastical leaders to affirm or celebrate unity. This is not unity from below nor love as a warm feeling. Nor is it the unity of mere membership in an organization. It is only a gift of God. Second, the essence of this community of relationship is love: love is to be the essence of the mutual indwelling in the triune God, as well as the essence of human relationships. There is no external code or other criterion that binds Christians together in uniformity. Nor is there a need for conformity. The disciples are not re-created as clones. Rather, the prayer is that their diversity may be expressed in the unity that exists in the unity and diversity of the Holy Trinity. The only criterion is love, the binding agency, as it were, of the Trinity, which holds them together. Third, if love is the binding agency, then this intimacy between Christians finds expression in the love they have for each other. "By this," Jesus says, "everyone will know that you are my disciples, if you have love for one another" (13:35). It is into this kind of intimacy that the disciples are invited to enter. Christians are to experience the unity in love that exists between Father and Son. This is possible through the indwelling of the Spirit.

## 2.2. Theosis: "May They Also Be in Us" (17:21)

Even mutuality among Christians does not exhaust the meaning and significance of this invitation. Christians are invited to participate in the very mutuality of the triune God.[194] Here we come to the heart of a great mystery. We can just about understand "Christ in us, the hope of glory." But this seems different. This is human participation in the divine. It is the mystery that lies behind the sacraments of the Church and the sense of the Holy in our midst. It is also what is expressed by other New Testament writers in slightly different ways. Paul, for example, states that Christians are called into the fellowship of His Son (κοινωνίαν τοῦ υἱοῦ αὐτοῦ Ἰησοῦ Χριστοῦ), Jesus Christ our Lord (1 Cor. 1:9). His favorite phrase is "in Christ." For the Petrine tradition, it is becoming participants of the divine nature (γένησθε θείας κοινωνοὶ φύσεως—2 Pet. 1:4). Both use the term *koinonia*, which has come into popular theology as a way of describing the fellowship that exists in the Church between believers. Important though this meaning may be, the focus in these passages is not on the fellowship of believers but on fellowship with the triune God. How are we to understand this? The primary model for us is, once again, the Incarnation. Here we have the human and the divine mutually interpenetrated, all in and through the Spirit.

Eastern Christianity has long spoken of the mystery of triune life using the image of the dance, with the Greek word *perichoresis* used as a metaphor that suggests "moving around, making room, relation to one another without losing identity."[195] It is into this dance that Christians are invited to enter. Our participation, of course, is by God's initiative and is therefore somewhat asymmetrical[196] since God always initiates.

But if we cannot explain the mystery, can we at least suggest some of its implications? The fourth Gospel itself offers us a few points. First, in this mutuality, we are utterly dependent upon the source of all life (1:3; 5:25-29; 6:52-57; 12:25), for the life we now live we live in Him. God's grace and initiative through the Atonement (more on this in a moment) is the source of our salvation. Second, this life of intimacy may be characterized as a life of joy. Earlier John has drawn attention to the eschatological dimension of joy in the face of the pain they are to experience, but he promises that their joy will be complete. Now in 17:13 he prays that their joy may be complete since he is coming to the Father. In essence, the completion of his work makes possible the joy of the believers who are now able to join in the intimacy of the divine relationship.[197] Third, just as Jesus did the works of His Father (4:17; 5:17, 19-21, 30), so we will also do these works, including belief in the One who sent the Son (6:28-29). Indeed, the works that we will do will be greater than those Jesus himself has done because He is going to the Father and the Spirit will be upon all (14:11-12). These works are part of the big purposes of God, part of the mission of God in the created order, rather than any self-centered or self-serving demands that sometimes lie behind "claiming this promise." And we are to exercise the prerogatives of God in carrying out this mission, surely the meaning of the often ignored reference to forgiveness of sins in 20:23. This implies that, as part of this theotic relationship, we know the mind of God in these matters and are able to speak with the confidence that comes from being intimately related to the triune God. Finally, we have a confidence born, not of our own strength, but of the peace and protection that is offered in the very being of God (16:33; 17:11, 15).

It is also important to say what *theosis* and *perichoresis* are not. As Pinnock states,

> There is no absorption of the person in God. By the grace of God and *as creatures* we participate in him. United to Christ without becoming Christ, we are also united to God without becoming God. . . . This is a personal union, not an ontological union. . . . As the Persons of the Trinity dwell in and with one another, so we, created in the image of God, dwell in and with one another, sharing the life of the Trinity and experiencing movements of love passing between the Persons.[198]

We always remain created creatures of God who participate in the life of God, rather than being absorbed into the being of God.

## 3. SANCTIFICATION

### 3.1. In the Truth: "Sanctify Them in the Truth; Your Word Is Truth" (17:17)

At last we come to a crucial verse and a favorite term: "sanctify." Sometimes this verse has been taken to mean that Jesus prays for the future work of grace through the Holy Spirit for the cleansing and empowering of the disciples at Pentecost. But important though that concept might be in general terms, it is a doubtful understanding of this passage. In John, the disciples are already clean. According to 15:3, "You have already been cleansed by the word that I have spoken to you." Not surprisingly, this seems to be a condition for abiding in the vine, the theme of John 15:1-8.[199] This, however, is not the meaning in John 17. Rather, it again seems to be a presupposition.

The context of 17:17 is a lengthy section in which Jesus prays for the protection of His disciples from the world. They have been called out of the world and He has guarded them by His teaching and care during His ministry. Now that His departure is near, He prays for their continued safety in the world. In the fourth Gospel, the world has a double significance. It is, on the one hand, a place and a mind-set of hostility to God and His purpose as revealed in Jesus' person and work. This hostility is at least partly due to the fact that the world is subject to the evil one. On the other hand, the world was created by the triune God and is the object of His love and mission: "For God so loved the world that he sent his only Son" (3:16). But Jesus is not praying for their removal from the world. If they are really to be Jesus' disciples, they cannot be taken out of the world. Instead He asks His Father "to protect them from the evil one" (17:15). They will need to be protected while they are in the world, completely involved in God's mission to His world.

In this context, then, "to sanctify" the disciples means to keep them safe from the hostility of the world and the power of the evil one, and to keep them on mission. They will be protected in the truth, in contrast to the big lie of the evil one (see 8:44-47). The active word of God that Jesus taught is the truth and is embodied in the One who is the Word made flesh and the One who is "the way, and the truth, and the life" (14:6). The point, then, is not the correct philosophical meaning of "the Truth"—remember Pilate's deliberate attempt to deflect the thrust of Jesus' pointed discussion with the great philosophical question, "What is truth?" (18:38). Jesus seems to play on the twofold meaning of "truth" here. On the one hand, He is the way, the truth, and the life, and they are sanctified in relationship to Him. It is also the understanding of who God is and His purposes in Christ as the way to life. Hence, they are sanctified by belief in Jesus, another way of speaking of abiding in Him (15:3-4) and the One who sent Him.

### 3.2. By the Sanctifying of the Son: "I Sanctify Myself, So That They Also May Be Sanctified" (17:19)

According to John, the disciples are sanctified by the sanctifying of the Son. Here it is important to ask just what the Johannine Jesus means when He says "for their sakes I sanctify myself" (ἐγὼ ἁγιάζω ἐμαυτόν). Earlier in debate with "the Jews,"[200] Jesus had referred to himself as "the one whom the Father has sanctified and sent into the world" (10:36). This cannot mean that He was purified or set apart for God's work—He and His Father have been working since eternity. More likely it has to do with the Incarnation and His undertaking the mission of God.[201] Confirmation of this view may be gained from the fact that this prayer concludes the so-called Upper Room Discourse placed just before the Crucifixion. In the fourth Gospel, the hour of Jesus' glorification is none other than the hour of His death. In His death, the righteous seeking purpose of God's holiness in drawing His lost creatures back to himself is fulfilled (see 12:27-32). Thus, the sanctification about which the Johannine Jesus speaks has nothing to do with any personal need for Jesus' forgiveness or cleansing and everything to do with the ultimate purposes of God. Jesus' prayer is that the disciples might indeed share that holiness, be kept in that relationship with the holy God, and share in God's mission. They are kept in His holy name (17:11), sanctified in the truth (v. 17), and kept in love (v. 26). Their sanctification is part of the whole notion of mutuality and indwelling to which we have devoted so much time in this chapter.

## 4. THE PURPOSE OF SANCTIFICATION

Finally, we come to the purpose of sanctification in this section of the fourth Gospel.[202] Popular holiness teaching often focuses upon the notion of heart purity and moral rectitude, sometimes linked with a view that holiness must lead to separation from the world in order to avoid contamination. But if these ideas are at all present in the fourth Gospel, they are certainly not prominent. Separation is important in the fourth Gospel, but it is not insulation from the world. Rather, it is essentially mission related.

A key assumption of this book has been that Christian holiness is *always* derived, utterly dependent upon our relationship to the holy God. As we have already seen, in the fourth Gospel, this relationship to the holy God is seen in terms of the mutuality and the relationality of the Trinity. The mutuality of the Holy Trinity has always been outward-looking, creative, and redemptive love.[203] Here the fourth Gospel is particularly clear—it is because "God so loved the world that he gave his only Son" (3:16). God, whose holiness is expressed through His seeking love, has made it possible for His alienated creation to be brought back into that intended relationship with Him. God's seeking love is the heart of the Christian gospel.

The consequences in history of the mutuality between Father and Son have been repeatedly noted in the fourth Gospel: Jesus does the work of the Father, fulfilling His purposes in the world and acting in complete unity with the Father. The consequences of mutuality for the disciples are the same. If the holiness of the triune God is manifest in His seeking love, the holiness of those who dwell in Him will find expression in love for each other. Keeping the love commandment is the primary way in which the world will know of this mutual indwelling. It also explains why the love commandment is the only demand laid upon the disciples (see 16:12-17). Christian holiness is thus a social, not an individual, phenomenon.

At first glance, this love commandment might seem to issue in a rather ingrown, self-centered "us-versus-them" kind of love. But that kind of love would not replicate the love in the Holy Trinity. Although the Trinity is complete in itself, God has from eternity freely chosen to love outside the Trinity. The love in the triune God has always been outward-looking, never self-absorbed. The outward-looking characteristic of the love relationship in the Holy Trinity is to be replicated in the disciples: As the Father sends the Son, so the Son sends the disciples (see 17:18). Just as the Father sanctified the Son and sent Him into the world (10:36; 3:16), Jesus sanctifies His disciples and sends them into the world. The Trinitarian shape of their mission is seen especially in 20:21-23: "Jesus said to them again, 'Peace be with you. As the Father has sent me, so I send you.' When he had said this, he breathed on them and said to them, 'Receive the Holy Spirit. If you forgive the sins of any, they are forgiven them; if you retain the sins of any, they are retained." In other words, believers are sanctified for service.

Thus, the sanctification of the disciples has a threefold purpose: to enable them to enter into and live in that relationship with God, which was intended from the beginning; to make them one with each other in love (17:23), and to enable them to act as agents of that reconciliation in the world (see v. 21). Jesus' followers are to reflect the character of God that is expressed in the loving commitment of disciples to one another. But it cannot stop there: mission is the clear goal of Christian holiness, of sanctification, not an inward-looking love.

## 5. ASPECTS OF HOLINESS IN JOHN

We may now draw together some of the implications of our discussion by restating some key points. First, God is a triune, social being of relationality, a perpetual movement of love. God's love is always outward-going rather than inward-looking. Second, creation itself is an expression of God's outward-looking love. Humanity is created in God's image, which means that the God-designed destiny of humans was to be in relationship—with the rest of the created order, with fellow human beings, and with the triune God. Third, the Fall marred all relationships: God and His creatures, a relationship that was damaged beyond human repair by our search for independence and desire to be our own god; male/female; humans/creation.

But God's salvific love has changed all of that. The disciples of Jesus are invited to experience the kind of unity that exists in God. Since the essence of this community of relationship is love, that is to be the essence of human relationships. Christians are to experience the unity in love that exists between Father and Son. Restoration of the image of God in humanity is essentially a restoration of marred relationships. We are also invited to participate in the very mutuality of the triune God. The primary model for us is, once again, the Incarnation. Here we have the human and the divine mutually interpenetrated, all in and through the Spirit. For us, however, this is a personal union, not an ontological union. In this mutuality, we are utterly dependent upon the source of all life. Just as Jesus did the works of His Father, so we will also do greater than those Jesus himself has done because He is going to the Father and the Spirit will be upon all (14:11-12). Thus we have a confidence born, not of our own strength, but of the peace and protection that is offered in the very being of God (16:33; 17:11, 15).

Sanctification of the disciples, therefore, includes keeping them safe from the hostility of the world and the power of the evil one and keeping them on mission. This mission is the ultimate purpose of the holy God. Jesus' prayer is that the disciples might indeed share that holiness, be kept in that relationship with the holy God, and share in God's mission. Thus, the sanctification of the disciples has a threefold purpose: to enable them to enter into and remain in that relationship with God which was intended from the beginning, to make them one with each other in love, and to enable them to act as agents of that reconciliation in the world. In sum, according to John, love is the expression of sanctification.

# 4

# HOLINESS AND DISCIPLESHIP
## THE GOSPEL OF MARK

◆

If holiness is a major biblical doctrine, one should expect to see it represented in all strands of biblical literature. In the previous chapters we saw the importance of the Incarnate Christ, full of the Spirit and living as a human among people, living in obedience to His Father through the power of the Spirit. We then explored the mystery of the Trinity, with *perichoresis* and *theosis* as helps to understanding the relationship into which disciples are invited. At least in these chapters, we ran into some familiar language—"filled with the Spirit," "sanctification," and so forth. But that brings us face-to-face with an uncomfortable fact: the Gospel of Mark seems to say very little about holiness, with no holiness terminology, no sanctification language at all. Is this a serious deficiency that should encourage us to bypass Mark for these purposes?

I think not. In chapter 1, we noted that the *story* of Jesus and the disciples in the Gospels gives us *theological* assistance. We have already seen how fruitful such an approach is through looking at parts of the Gospel of Luke. The Gospels, in short, have a theological value that parallels their importance as our sources for information about Jesus' life and teaching. We also reminded ourselves that the Gospels have relevance for post-Pentecost Christians even if they tell the story of Jesus and His disciples before Pentecost.

Although Mark does not use the terminology of sanctification, he does have a lot to say about discipleship. What if the story of Jesus and His disciples actually is another way of talking about the life of holiness? If this is so, then, the Gospel of Mark, far from being devoid of holiness material, contains a very rich vein indeed. Or, to put it another way, if the Markan model for the holy life is following Jesus, what are its salient features? Mark's story of Jesus and His disciples taken as a whole might help us in our quest.

One little point: if we emphasize discipleship as the way of holiness, might there not be a danger that grace would be eclipsed and we end up with "works righteousness"? It must be admitted that such fears are well-founded if the legalism that bedevils some "holiness people" is the practical outworking of their theology. If *holiness* is reduced to *morality,* that is, to a moral code to be followed, legalism is almost inevitable. But if holiness is always *life lived in response to a relationship,* the danger of "works righteousness" evaporates. Sometimes those who hold to a static view of salvation involving primarily a legal concept of the Atonement find discipleship and obedience difficult to accommodate within their salvation story. They all too readily collapse the path of discipleship into its starting point. But if we avoid a static view of justification and sanctification[204] and, instead, think of the relational character of God's righteousness, then the problems of "merit" and "works" tend to be minimized. Understood relationally, justification and sanctification are dynamic, not the opposite of discipleship but very much like discipleship.

## 1. "THE HOLY ONE OF GOD"[205]

Many people thought that Jesus was an eschatological prophet (8:28) announcing that the time of the longed-for restoration has dawned, the time of fulfillment has arrived (1:14-15). Clearly, Jesus' message *is* radical and He *is* announcing the arrival of the kingdom of God (v. 15),[206] but Jesus is more than the eschatological prophet announcing the end time.

The beginning of Mark is especially important for the identity of Jesus. For Mark, Jesus is the One who is the bearer *and* the content of the Good News. From the outset, Mark wishes his readers to know that the rest of the Gospel is about "Jesus Christ, the Son of God" (see v. 1). But this identity is more complex than we might first imagine. It takes the rest of the Gospel to work out exactly what Mark conveys by his opening lines.

Jesus' identification is confirmed in a constellation of images and metaphors within the story. First, the announcement of the baptist picks up the Isaianic theme of "restoration eschatology."[207] According to 1:4, the Baptist is "the voice of one crying out in the wilderness." Although the wilderness is almost certainly a geographical location, it has significance beyond that.[208] The wilderness is the place through which the returning remnant from the Babylonian exile travel. According to Isa. 35:8, the Lord makes a way of holiness in the wilderness on which the unclean cannot travel nor wild beasts cause harm. Mark's citation of Isa. 40:3 and the deliberate location of John in the wilderness evokes the entire holy remnant notion. John calls the people to repent and be baptized, thus creating a holy people fit for a holy God. His role is to gather together "the remnant of Israel destined for salvation."[209] This is the beginning of the re-creation of the people of God.

The response to John's preaching is a renewal of the people of God who are coming *from Jerusalem and Judea and* are coming *into the wilderness* to be baptized by John. But John's is still a preparatory role. He fulfills the task of Elijah[210] as the forerunner before Jesus' face, the one who sets the stage for Jesus Messiah, Son of God, the Holy One of God. Now the restored holy people of God are ready for the mightier one to baptize them with the Holy Spirit and lead them on His mission. The eschatological time-scale has been altered. Jesus announces the arrival of the kingdom of God: the time is *now* and John's work is the opening scene (see 1:1). In short, the kingdom of God has arrived in the coming of Jesus. That, Mark tells us, is inaugurated when Jesus arrives in Galilee after John is arrested. In sum, Mark begins his Gospel by recasting the story of Israel, making it the story of Jesus, Son of God, and of His people.

Second, Jesus is the One on whom the Spirit descends (1:10). Right at the beginning of His ministry, we have an implicit Trinitarian focus, with Jesus, the Spirit, and the voice from heaven all in the same scene. According to Mark, Jesus assumes His mission without any prehistory set out in birth narratives. This has led to suggestions that Mark has an adoptionist Christology, but the unfolding narrative seriously undermines any such view.[211] Jesus, at His baptism,[212] undertakes the mission of God. Jesus sees the heavens open and the Spirit descending like a dove on Him and He hears the voice from heaven confirm that He is indeed the beloved Son, chosen and royal (v. 11).[213] The descent of the Spirit on Jesus identifies Him as the locale of God among His people.[214] The temptation by Satan in the wilderness puts Jesus' obedience to the test (vv. 12-13), signaling the depth of opposition that He will encounter along the way.[215] But the tempter is thwarted and Jesus returns proclaiming the good news of God. The confrontation with Satan together with this encounter with the demoniac are sharp reminders that the struggle for God's rule is ultimately cosmic rather than mundane. It is clear that the opposition knows who it is up against.[216]

The third thread of identity in Mark 1 comes from a most unusual source.[217] After choosing His first disciples, Jesus encounters a man with an unclean spirit in the synagogue at Capernaum. When the unclean spirit sees Jesus, he bears reluctant, but confirming, testimony to Jesus' identity: "I know who you are, the Holy One of God" (v. 24). This phrase is not prominent in terms of use, but it is crucial in its placement and meaning.[218] When considered in its narrative context and juxtaposed to the coalesced images in Mark, it is an important ingredient in Mark's motif of the renewed holy people of God centered on Jesus and His disciples.

Several literary observations signal its importance. First, the fact that the phrase "the Holy One of God" in verse 24 is placed on the lips of an unclean spirit points to the term's accuracy. Mark takes it for granted that the unclean spirits have true knowledge of the unseen world that remains hidden from the mundane world.[219] The unclean spirit gives an identity to Jesus of which those around are unaware, an impression confirmed by Jesus' command that the unclean spirit be silent (v. 25). In fact, according to a general comment in 3:11, Mark notes that "whenever the unclean spirits saw him, they fell down before him and shouted, 'You are the Son of God!'" Mark considers this to be their routine identification of Jesus. The phrase the "Holy One of God" is a subset of "Son of God."

In turn, two "Son of God" ascriptions occur in Mark. At the trial scene in 14:61 the high priest asks, "Are you the Messiah, the Son of the Blessed One?"[220] At one level, this twofold identification stays within conventional second Temple images for Messiah and Son of the Blessed One. The response of the Markan Jesus moves beyond both descriptions through the evocative phrase ἐγώ εἰμι ("I am") as well as equating Messiah with the suffering Son of Man figure already established in 8:27-32. The second linked identity occurs at the Crucifixion. In 15:39, the centurion in attendance at the Cross says, "Truly this man was son of God."[221] For Mark the term connotes far more than could be gleaned from an analysis of its background in the second Temple period.[222] In both of these instances, the confessions are true for Mark, but the speakers in the story do not have the same understanding.

These pointers to Jesus' identity all come from reluctant witnesses. No such reluctance attaches to the final two cognate identifications in Mark. According to 1:10-11, Jesus sees "the heavens torn apart and the Spirit descending like a dove on him. And a voice came from heaven, 'You are my Son, the Beloved.'"[223] In this first instance, this identification is for Jesus himself. According to Mark, Jesus alone sees the rending of the heavens and hears the voice identifying and affirming His mission. In the Transfiguration story (9:3-10), the voice is for the three disciples—and because of His identity, they are to listen to Him.

Son of God is a key term right from the opening lines of the Gospel. Mark begins by telling his readers that the whole narrative[224] is about Jesus Christ, the Son of God.[225] The phrase forms an inclusio with the words of the centurion in 15:39, which serve as literary markers enclosing the bulk of Mark's narrative, indicating that Mark intends to develop through the story precisely what he means by "Son of God."

The identity of Jesus is crucial for the point Mark intends to make about discipleship. Through the subtle use of Old Testament allusions and highlighting the descent of the Holy Spirit on Jesus, Mark shows us that Jesus is now the locale of God among His people. He is actually the Holy One in their midst, bringing the end time to pass. The implications of that belief are enormous.

## 2. THE CALL AND IDENTITY OF DISCIPLES[226] (1:16—3:34)

All scholars agree that Mark's Gospel focuses upon Jesus. But most also acknowledge that a major subtheme is teaching on discipleship.[227] Our concern in this chapter is primarily with the latter theme.

Immediately[228] after the identity of Jesus is established (1:9-13), Mark gives a summary of the message of Jesus (vv. 14-15). This preaching about the kingdom of God[229] follows after the temptation, which, in turn, is followed by the selection of the first disciples (vv. 16-20). Clearly, the announcing and effecting of God's rule requires a people called to embody and proclaim this Good News (see Exod. 19:6).

Mark does not give any details about these first disciples.[230] They simply respond to the call to follow Him, leave their nets—no halfhearted commitment for them—and set out for an unannounced destination. They follow with a blank check, as it were.[231] It is only when we get to chapter 3 where Mark tells of the more comprehensive call of the Twelve that we get a little more information. Jesus appoints 12 to be with Him and to be sent out to preach and to have authority over the demons (3:14-15).

The disciples are called to be with Jesus, empowered by Him and on His mission (v. 14). The juxtapositioning of the identity of Jesus and the call to be with Him cannot be merely accidental. These disciples are called by the Holy One and brought into a relationship with Him. The number of disciples—12—clearly has a historical basis since it occurs in all the Gospels. But this is almost certainly another echo from the Old Testament, suggesting that Jesus thinks of the Twelve as a representative group of the people of God.[232] By being with the Holy One of God, they are representing the people of God, a holy nation with the Holy One of God dwelling in their midst. When they are on His mission, they are acting as the people of God, a kingdom of priests. In sum, *discipleship and the call to be holy are inextricably linked.*

But Mark also wants to identify those who are disciples in a different way. Just after Jesus appoints the Twelve, He returns home (v. 19). The reception He receives is decidedly mixed. The crowds are everywhere; His family is greatly concerned (v. 21).

The narrative context of this story is most interesting. Since chapter 2, the religious authorities have shown a growing anxiety about Jesus leading ultimately to outright hostility. Opposition comes first from the scribes. They think that Jesus is a blasphemer because He claims to speak for God by forgiving sins (2:6). Then the scribes of the Pharisees object to the company Jesus keeps because He welcomes sinners to himself (v. 16). The Pharisees themselves question Jesus' right to set aside the Sabbath regulations (v. 23). This debate finally leads to a conspiracy between the Pharisees, a separatist holiness movement, and the Herodians, rather strange bedfellows indeed (3:6). This opposition occurs in the face of Jesus' teaching and deeds, all signs of the Kingdom's presence.

The story itself[233] starts with the family seeking to restrain Jesus because people were saying, "He has gone out of his mind" (v. 21). The *scribes from Jerusalem* explain Jesus' activity by saying that He is actually in opposition to God—He is doing the work of Satan. This, of course, is the conclusion they have already drawn from their assessment of Jesus in relation to the big questions, "Who speaks for God?" and "On what grounds does God accept sinners?"[234] Jesus' answer to their assertion is significant. First, He points to the absurdity of their explanation: "How can anything survive when the opposition is internal?"[235] Second, although all sins, even blasphemy, are forgivable,[236] by opposing God's purposes worked through the Spirit, they put themselves beyond the pale. The story then returns to the family, who are now "standing outside" (v. 31), indeed, "are outside" (v. 32), asking for Him.

The whole section from 2:1 to 3:34 is full of irony. Through their failure to recognize the presence of the Kingdom in Jesus, those originally inside, the religious leaders and even the family of Jesus, have resolutely moved outside and become those to whom everything is in parables that they fail to grasp (see 4:11-12). Those originally on the outside—the sinners, the blemished, the demonized, the crowds, and the disciples—are now on the inside. The narrative concludes by having Jesus say to the crowd sitting around Him, *Whoever does the will of God is my brother and sister and mother* (3:35). The family of God is not genetically determined nor restricted to an inner circle.

## 3. THE JOURNEY OF DISCIPLESHIP

Jesus has the disciples with Him from Galilee to the Cross; they are being taught through word and deed throughout the time they are traveling with Him. To put it another way, discipleship in Mark involves a journey. We cannot possibly discuss the entire journey here, but we can give "edited highlights" that indicate aspects of Mark's theology.

### 3.1. Clues to Jesus' Identity (4:1—8:21)

The unfolding story of Jesus and His disciples is full of clues about the identity of this man who is the Holy One of God in their midst. But this identity is only open to those who have eyes to see and ears to hear (4:11; 8:17-18). Not only is Jesus teaching in parables, but His deeds are also parabolic and therefore obscure to those who have hardened their hearts against Him.

When all the details of the picture are put together, it seems perfectly obvious to us that the disciples are, at the very least, dim and, at worst, positively antagonistic. After all, the clues come thick and fast throughout the narrative. (Isn't hindsight a wonderful gift?) Jesus is pictured as the Master Teacher, patiently explaining the kingdom of God to the disciples in private (4:1-34) and explaining the true meaning of purity in contrast to the external rules of holiness as handed down in the traditions of the elders

(7:1-23). He is also the Master of creation, stilling the storm when the disciples panic and coming to them in the midst of the storm, bringing peace to their distress (4:38-41; 6:45-56). He who has met Satan and withstood his temptations, now confronts the powers, exorcising demons from those who were possessed.

Jesus is also pictured as the liberator of the marginalized. He heals lepers, excluded from normal society; casts out Legion from the man who lives among the tombs; heals a woman with an issue of blood, which kept her in a perpetual state of uncleanness, and therefore unable to participate in the corporate worship of the people of God. He even touches a corpse in order to restore life, thus personally incurring corpse impurity while at the same time signaling the liberating power of the Kingdom even over death. Even Gentiles benefit from His gracious provision, with the Syrophoenician woman's daughter liberated from demonic oppression (7:24-28) and the deaf and dumb man enabled to hear and speak clearly (vv. 31-37).[237]

Jesus also cares for those who are scattered like sheep without a shepherd (6:34). He feeds the 5,000 in Israel (vv. 30-44) with sufficient left over to symbolize the care for all of Israel; He follows that with a feeding in Gentile territory (8:1-10) with sufficient left over to symbolize the care for the entire Gentile world. As Lord of creation, messianic healer, liberator, teacher, and sustainer, His writ runs to the entire created order, animate and inanimate. Echoes from Scripture abound.

When we come to the end of this section, then, we are astonished when the Pharisees ask Him for a sign from heaven (v. 11). No wonder Mark tells us that Jesus "sighed deeply in his spirit" (v. 12). Surely all that has gone before will be a sufficient sign for the disciples, if not the Pharisees.

Apparently not! The next little episode in verses 14-21 is remarkable for its candor. The disciples and Jesus are on another boat ride. Jesus decides to take the opportunity to warn them against following the Pharisees and Herodians in their opposition to Him. Jesus, of course, puts His teaching in the form of a cryptic saying: "Beware of the yeast of the Pharisees and the yeast of

Herod" (v. 15). The disciples look in puzzlement at each other and say, "What's He on about now? Oh, I get it! He knows that we have only one loaf in the boat and wonders what we will do when it comes time to eat" (see v. 16). When Jesus becomes aware of their little private conversation, He is scathing, reminding them of the two miraculous feedings that they have not only seen but in which they have been active participants. "Do you not yet understand?" He demands of them (v. 21).

What an astonishing story. The disciples have been through numerous pointers to the presence of the Kingdom. They have even participated in Jesus' mission of teaching and healing (see 6:7-13, 30-31). But they still have not really understood who He is. Is it any wonder that the Markan Jesus embarks now upon a sustained journey of teaching the disciples while they are "on the way"?

## 3.2. Teaching the Disciples on the Way (8:22—10:52)

This central section contains extensive teaching on discipleship. Two stories bracket the teaching. First is the unique Markan two-stage healing (8:22-26); at the end is the healing of blind Bartimaeus (10:46-52).

Jesus and His disciples are also on a journey from Caesarea Philippi to Jerusalem. Peter confesses that Jesus is Messiah in Caesarea Philippi, in Gentile territory and near the northern extent of Jesus' ministry. They then begin the long journey to Jerusalem, and it is on the way that the disciples are taught the meaning of true Messiahship and the cost of following that Messiah in true discipleship. The journey, then, is theological as well as geographical.[238]

The first healing is placed just after Jesus' despairing remark about the disciples' complete lack of understanding. They are spiritually blind and deaf (see 6:52; 8:17). Almost certainly Mark wants his readers to know that only a miracle of grace, the touch by Jesus, can give the disciples sight. But this will not be an easy process. Only gradually will they have their sight fully restored. Mark thereby sets the scene for the remainder of this central section of the Gospel.

Some holiness preachers in the past have seen in this story a good example of the second work of grace. Clearly, grace is required to give sight. Experience and Scripture alike confirm that few of us understand fully right from the start. The gracious touch and teaching of Jesus will be required for all disciples to come to a full knowledge and understanding of who Jesus is. For some, their experience of God's grace in their lives bears remarkable correspondence to this two-stage healing. But the significance of this story is not in the sequence of salvation but in the subsequent narrative.

Immediately following this healing story in 8:22-26, the disciples are asked the identity of Jesus: "Who do people say that I am?" (v. 27). They tell Him what the people believe, but Jesus presses them further: "Who do you say that I am?"[239] Peter says, "You are the Messiah" (v. 29). The penny has finally dropped. A great deal of the tension in the narrative disappears. At last, we think, they understand. The confession represents something of a watershed for them and in the Gospel story itself.

It is immediately clear, however, that their knowledge remains strictly limited. They understand who Jesus is, but they do not know what it means for either the Messiah or His followers. Because He understands the cultural context in which they have made this confession, Jesus immediately forbids them to tell anyone that He is the Messiah. Instead, He tells them that the Son of Man must suffer (v. 31). To be Messiah, therefore, is to be a suffering Son of Man kind of Messiah.

Peter, however, has other ideas. He is clearly reflecting the views of others and the standard hopes of those waiting for God to act during this period of second Temple Judaism. A suffering Son of Man is not their idea of a messiah. He therefore remonstrates with Jesus, telling Him this cannot be the way for the Messiah to go. But Jesus, in turn, rebukes Peter, stating that he has put himself on the side of the opposition to God—and is actually acting like Satan in his attempt to turn Jesus from His God-ordained path (vv. 32-33).

At that point, Jesus takes the whole discussion further: "He called the crowd with his disciples, and said to them: 'If any want to become my followers, let them deny themselves and take up their cross and follow me" (v. 34). There are two points to note here. First, this call is issued, not just to the inner circle, the Twelve, but to all who would follow Jesus. He invites the crowds to follow Him. No two-tier discipleship here. Second, discipleship is all or nothing. No partial commitment or part-time discipleship is on offer. It's cross-bearing servanthood for them all, even to death. "Those who want to save their life will lose it, and those who lose their life for my sake, and for the sake of the gospel, will save it" (v. 35). The disciples, however, find this very hard to understand and to accept. They still have a long way to go on their theological journey.

The next episode is the Transfiguration. The placement of this episode here has puzzled many scholars.[240] But the reason becomes clearer when read in the wider context. Jesus began His mission with the voice from heaven (1:11), which confirmed His identity and mission, followed immediately by the test of His obedience. After a host of clues to His identity, His disciples have finally learned who He is. But Jesus has had to tell them in no uncertain terms that their expectations are a long way from the path laid out for Him, and for any who would be His followers. The Transfiguration confirms Jesus' identity again and, by implication, His path and that of those who would follow Him. Jesus alone hears the "voice from heaven" the first time (vv. 10-11): this time, three disciples also hear it, although Peter's response shows that they still haven't grasped the whole point of it.[241]

The placement of the story is hardly accidental. Jesus has just been identified as "Messiah" by Peter in 8:27-30 and has immediately reinterpreted that confession in terms of a suffering Son of Man (v. 31). Peter finds this objectionable leading, in turn, to a rebuke from Jesus. Then, in the immediately preceding pericope, Jesus calls the crowd along with the disciples to follow Him in cross-bearing. The voice from the cloud is a pointed reminder to the three that Jesus' message is God's message. If they wish to set their minds on divine rather than human things, they will need to listen to Jesus, the Son of Man. The path of cross-bearing servanthood is the path God has laid out for Jesus and His followers.

When the group returns from the Mount of Transfiguration, they are confronted with a botched exorcism (9:14-29). Earlier, the disciples were sent out on mission two by two and Jesus "gave them authority over the unclean spirits. . . . So they went out and proclaimed that all should repent. They cast out many demons, and anointed with oil many who were sick and cured them" (6:7, 12-13). Then they were successful. What has changed?

The clue comes at the end of the story when Jesus tells the disciples, "This kind can come out only through prayer" (9:29). Physical separation from Jesus cannot be the reason. After all, they have been apart from Him before (see 6:6-13). Nor can it be a matter of technique.[242] A further clue comes 10 verses later, where Mark places an interesting story about John bar Zebedee. He has John say to Jesus, "Teacher, we saw someone casting out demons in your name, and we tried to stop him, because he was not following us" (9:38). Now the problem becomes clearer: the disciples may have begun to see themselves as independently empowered exorcists, perhaps on a level with Jesus himself.[243] Jesus reminds them that this unknown exorcist was doing a deed of power in His name (v. 39). That was the crucial point, success is dependent upon the name of Jesus, not whether He had the imprimatur of the disciples. The failed exorcism, then, could well be attributed to their growing sense of self-reliance rather than utter dependence upon God in Christ. The mission of disciples is always God's, and they are always utterly dependent upon Him for its success.

But this was far from the only lesson they need to learn. The journey continues through Galilee, and along the way, Jesus makes His second passion prediction. Once again, the disciples do not understand and are afraid to ask (vv. 30-32). But instead of opposing Him to His face as they had done after the first prediction, this time they are arguing with one another about who is the greatest. The contrast between Jesus and His disciples is stark. Understanding still lags significantly behind following. Jesus, the Teacher, tells them that the first will be last and the last first (vv. 33-37).

Other lessons are given in Judea.[244] Here Jesus teaches them about the need to forsake the rights of Jewish males, the status of an adult, and the dependence upon security for the incomparable rights, status, and security of the kingdom of God. This teaching leaves the disciples perplexed, and they respond to His teaching on the problem of wealth with the pointed question, "Then who can be saved?" (10:26). The question is not an idle one, for it shows just how difficult it is to abandon rights, security, and status. In fact, Jesus' response is that "for mortals it is impossible, but not for God; for God all things are possible" (v. 27). Jesus then reminds His disciples of the incomparable rights, status, and security of the Kingdom, both now and in the future. But discipleship will also include persecution (vv. 29-31), a line often missed in reading Mark, not least by Matthew and Luke![245] Just to emphasize that point, Jesus then gives His third and most detailed passion prediction.

It might have been hoped that the disciples would have become more aware of the implications of following Jesus by this time. Alas, such seems not to have been the case. Just after this prediction, James and John try to put one over on the other disciples and ask Jesus to do something special for them. Jesus asks, "What is it you want me to do for you?" (v. 36), to which they respond by asking for the best seats in the Kingdom—Prime Minister and Chancellor of the Exchequer,[246] perhaps. Jesus, once again, reminds them of the role of cross-bearing servanthood that is to be theirs if they are to follow Him. The model of authority in the community of believers is to be radically different from that of the Gentile hierarchy with which they would be familiar. Their model was to be himself: "For the Son of Man did not came to be served but to serve, and to give his life a ransom for many" (v. 45).

Finally, they arrive at Jericho. Here the second of our two blind man stories is placed. Bartimaeus cries out for mercy from the Son of David. So Jesus asks him, in words almost identical to those asked of James and John, "What do you want me to do for you?" (v. 51). The blind man says, "My teacher, let me see again." Mark tells us that "immediately he regained his sight and followed him on the way" (vv. 51, 52).

### 3.3. The Summit of Discipleship Teaching (11:1—12:44)[247]

It should come as little surprise that Jesus' journey ends in the Temple or that His teaching reaches its pinnacle there. Two questions[248] addressed to Jesus by His opponents[249] confirm Him as the authoritative interpreter of the Scriptures. For our purposes, the second question (12:28-34) is the more important. A scribe asks for Jesus' opinion of the great commandments. Jesus summarizes them with the Shema of Deut. 6:4 and the call to love of neighbor from Lev. 19:18. The scribe, commending Jesus for His answer, then repeats the summary and adds that these two commandments count for much more than all burnt offerings and sacrifices.[250]

The significance of the scribe's response cannot be overestimated. These two commandments, the heart of second Temple Jewish piety, are at the center of Jesus' kingdom Torah, but because the Kingdom has arrived, the teaching has a much more radical and daring conclusion. The center of God's good purposes are to be found in the inward, in-the-heart Torah promised by Jeremiah and Ezekiel. That time has arrived: the purpose and goal to which the Temple and the whole people of God point but which have not been grasped, are now being proclaimed and effected in Jesus himself.[251] No wonder that Mark tells us, "After that no one dared ask him any question" (12:34).

### 3.4. Disciples and the Passion Narrative (13:1—16:8)

Mark 13 has always attracted attention,[252] not least because it points decidedly to the future. But Mark gives some hints that show how he intends his readers to understand this section. Although this concerns the fate of the Temple,[253] it is still discipleship-teaching[254] and is linked with the following passion narrative through a variety of continuing motifs.[255]

Jesus does not easily reach the point of predicting Temple

destruction. Jesus calls all of Israel to join the restoration movement (1:38; 2:17; 8:34) and to become part of the new people of God (3:35; 6:7-13; 10:23-31) because God's purposes for His world have entered a new and decisive stage (1:14-15). Mark also shows that there has been resistance almost from the beginning. Implacable opposition to Jesus leads to the passion narrative; the passion narrative leads to the destruction of the Temple. "For Mark, the destruction of the Temple represented both the natural political outcome of the Jewish refusal to follow Christ and the divine censure of that refusal."[256]

But Mark's purpose here is more pastoral than predictive.[257] He wants to teach His first readers "how to live as faithful disciples without knowing when the End will come."[258] Mark 13:32-37 shows that the point of chapter 13 is to encourage "discipleship and mission, discerning ears and eyes to detect God at work, and unfailing confidence that the kingdom, still hidden, is destined to be revealed."[259]

Perhaps the most important lesson on discipleship comes in the passion narrative itself. It centers on failure, rather than success.[260] The disciples have just finished the Last Supper with Jesus when they go to the Mount of Olives. There they listen to Jesus predict that they will all be deserters. Not surprisingly, this is a shock. "Peter said to him, 'Even though all become deserters, I will not.' . . . 'Even though I must die with you, I will not deny you.' And all of them said the same" (14:29, 31).

We all know the subsequent story well: just 20 short verses later, Mark writes, "All of them deserted him and fled" (v. 50). Peter's failure is outlined clearly. He is confronted by a slave girl (twice) and some bystanders and denies Jesus three times before realizing the enormity of his failure (vv. 53-72). But Jesus has also predicted, "After I am raised up, I will go before you to Galilee" (v. 28). According to 16:6-7, the young man at the tomb says to the women: "Do not be alarmed; you are looking for Jesus of Nazareth, who was crucified. He has been raised; he is not here. Look, there is the place they laid him. But go, tell his disciples and Peter that he is going ahead of you to Galilee; there you will see him, just as he told you."

It is hard to imagine a more important statement for the first disciples, and for Mark's readers, then and now. Peter, the one who has been so strong in his affirmation of loyalty, is also the one who plumbs the depths of denial.[261] But Jesus gathers the scattered flock of disciples together again, with the young man at the empty tomb especially singling out Peter. Despite his appalling failure, he has been restored to the journey and is invited to follow Jesus who is still going ahead of them.

## 4. ASPECTS OF HOLINESS IN MARK

And so the story ends.[262] It remains only for us to attempt to draw from the story a Markan theology of holiness. In sum, the Markan picture of the holy life is based completely upon an *ongoing relationship with the Holy One*. Human holiness is always derived, always in *relationship* to the Holy One. Through their identification with Jesus, the disciples are the holy people of God, in an *ongoing* relationship with Him. This relationship has a number of characteristics.

First, discipleship has a *starting point*. It comes in the call to follow Jesus. It may be the first encounter with Christ or it may come as a subsequent call after the first encounter (see 1:16-20; 3:13; 8:34). Discipleship is more than answering the call to be a disciple. Sole attention to the call makes discipleship into a static contract rather than an ongoing relationship. We need to be able to combine a decision once taken with a daily reenactment (see Mark 8:34 and the Lucan parallel). Mark does not have one single model for entering into discipleship (see 8:22-26; 10:46-52). The path of discipleship cannot be collapsed into this starting point.[263]

Second, discipleship is not an individual pursuit. The disciples are *in it together*. The call of the Twelve who are made into a group is instructive. The impression of these disparate persons being fashioned into the corporate representatives of the new people of God is strengthened by the Last Supper, their subsequent failure, and Jesus' reconstitution of them in Galilee at the end of the narrative. We need to think of discipleship as something we do together in following Jesus, not something that is done alone. "I come to the garden alone" does not really epitomize the path of discipleship.

Third, discipleship means being together *with Jesus on His mission.* The disciples are to proclaim and effect the kingdom of God in history. Like Jesus, they encounter opposition to the message, confronting evil on the mundane and spiritual level in exorcisms and effecting signs of the coming Kingdom in the relief of suffering. On this mission they are utterly dependent upon Jesus.

Fourth, discipleship is a journey that involves *full commitment right from the start* (see 1:20; 10:28): there is no partial discipleship in Mark (see 10:17 ff.). Full commitment does not require full understanding, of course. The disciples really don't know the details of their path. They are frequently confused, often blind, and sometimes just thick. Sometimes, a tension arises between understanding and following, but they still follow Jesus with a day-by-day commitment along the way.

Fifth, discipleship is *for all.* Mark is quite clear about this. The Twelve are but the first of the new people of God. To be sure, discipleship is not identical in expression for all who are called to follow Him (see 10:17 ff.; 15:41, 42-43). But cross-bearing servanthood is not just an option for the select few (see 8:33-38).

Sixth, the journey of discipleship is *open-ended* (see 1:16-20; 16:8). The end is not clear from the beginning. But even when the disciples are uncertain about where Jesus is taking them (8:33— 10:52), they still follow. That, of course, is also the message Mark has for his readers, especially if the Gospel ends at 16:8.

Seventh, the journey involves *progression, not unremitting positive growth.* There is progression in Mark, but sometimes it seems like "one step forward and two steps back." Quite frankly, on occasion the disciples are an embarrassment. They quarrel about greatness, position, and power when Jesus is speaking of His death. They begin to fancy themselves as independently empowered exorcists with exclusive rights for exorcism vested in "Jesus and the Disciples' Ministries Incorporated" (see 9:14-29,

38-41). They look but don't see; they listen but don't hear. They are admonished to keep awake (13:37; 14:34, 38), but when asked to watch and pray, they fall asleep (vv. 37, 40, 41). At the end of the journey, Peter and the others vow undying loyalty to Jesus in verse 29; before the chapter ends, they have all left Him, Peter is cursing at a slave girl and denying that he ever knew Jesus. Not an unmitigated success story.

Eighth, *even the most committed disciples may fail, even after being on the way with Jesus for some time.* This may be Mark's most important lesson to his readers, not least those of us in the Holiness Movement who sometimes give the impression that once we have committed ourselves wholly to God, sin and failure are past. Failure is not inevitable, of course, but it can occur if we don't "keep awake." Sometimes we underestimate the challenges we face; sometimes we simply fail to keep close to Jesus; sometimes we even deny we ever knew Him. Failure remains a lamentable possibility for committed disciples.

Ninth, *forgiveness and restoration are offered to failed disciples.* Grace and restoration, not failure and rejection, are Mark's last words to disciples who fail. The remorse Peter feels at his failure is captured by Mark in these words: "Then Peter remembered . . . And he broke down and wept" (v. 72). The explicit naming of Peter at the empty tomb reminds us of grace, forgiveness, and restoration for even the most appalling failure (see 3:28). To Mark's first readers as to us, this must come as a particular word of gospel.

Finally, Jesus' teaching comes to its high point with the reiteration of the Great Commandments. For Jesus, for Mark, and for Wesley, these two commandments sum up God's good purposes and Christian holiness. There is no hint, of course, that the disciples are able to fulfill these commands in their own strength. Discipleship in Mark is pictured as a human impossibility. But disciples still follow, still are committed to Jesus and His way, still trusting in His promise that God's good purposes will ultimately prevail for them and for God's entire created order.

"After that no one dared ask him any question" (12:34).

## 5

# "PERFECT LIKE YOUR FATHER"
## THE GOSPEL OF MATTHEW

Georg Strecker in his book *The Sermon on the Mount: An Exegetical Commentary* begins his discussion by observing that "no proper exegesis of the Sermon on the Mount can ignore the results of more than two hundred years of historical-critical research on the New Testament."[264] For Strecker, the key result is that the sermon in its present form is the literary work of the evangelist, not a speech by Jesus. This conclusion seems beyond serious challenge, although it is certainly conceivable that much of the teaching contained in the Sermon on the Mount goes back to the historical Jesus in one form or another. In our final chapter, our interest is in what Matthew might contribute to our understanding of Christian holiness.

Like Mark, Matthew seems to say very little about Christian holiness. But he does have that notoriously difficult command of Jesus: "Be perfect, therefore, as your heavenly Father is perfect" (5:48). This sounds like a requirement that is a worthy but quite unattainable goal and, hence, an irrelevancy.[265] Such a conclusion is problematic, but the verse does pose the question: "Just how holy does God expect and enable His people to be in this life?" in its sharpest form. Eventually, as the title to this chapter suggests, we shall come to this verse. But the groundwork for understanding must be laid carefully, lest it be dismissed as utopian or become a burden too great to bear.

## 1. THE LITERARY CONTEXT

Matthew is first in the New Testament canon. A canonical reading of the Bible tries to determine if there is any literary significance to the relationship between the juxtaposed segments.

Thus, the placement of Matthew after Malachi needs to be taken into consideration. If there is significance, we should expect to find in it some sort of emphasis upon the link or transition markers between the story in the Old Testament and its continuation in the New. That is precisely what we find. Matthew, more than any of the other evangelists, deliberately sets out to show the continuity of Jesus with the Old Testament.[266] Perhaps the clearest indication of this feature is the familiar Matthean formula indicating that *this was to fulfill what had been spoken by the Lord through the prophet.*[267]

Scholars have long been intrigued by the structure of Matthew.[268] Davies and Allison regard the pattern of alternative narrative and discourse with five major discourses, as firmly established.[269] A triadic structure of Matthew is also defended while Allison has provided a detailed analysis of the Sermon that supports this view.[270] Plan and purpose clearly underlie Matthew's structure, but understanding the literary context is far more than simply analyzing structure.[271]

As has been the case throughout this book in considering the other Gospels, the narrative sequence in Matthew is highly significant for understanding this text. Reflections on where Matthew has placed the sermon itself as well as its shape and the content may prove fruitful. Particularly for the sermon, establishing the identity of the person who is delivering it is essential if 5:48 is not to be misunderstood.[272] According to Matthew, who is this person who calls disciples to be perfect like their Father? And what does it mean? Consideration of the narrative setting is crucial for answering these questions.

## 1.1. The Birth Narratives

Both Matthew and Luke use birth narratives to fill in the landscape on which to paint the life and work of Jesus.[273] The narratives differ in detail.[274] Matthew's stories are particularly full of allusions to the Old Testament, which firmly establish his view that the story of Jesus is in some sense the fulfillment of the story of Israel.[275] Direct formula markers occur in 1:22; 2:5, 15, 17, 23, but allusions are present throughout.

Opening lines in novels are often memorable. Any English literature pupil or high school graduate, for example, would instantly know the source of Dickens' memorable sentence, "It was the best of times; it was the worst of times." But how many of us recall anyone reading Matt. 1:1-17 last Christmas? Who cares that "Perez" was "the father of Hezron," and that "Hezron" was "the father of Aram" (v. 3)? Matthew does, and his first (Jewish) readers would. There are some interesting stylistic aspects to the genealogy, including the number of families[276] and the structure of the genealogy.[277] But two key points come right at the beginning (v. 1: "an account of the genealogy of Jesus the Messiah, the son of David, the son of Abraham").

"Son of David" was, in second Temple Judaism, "a title for the messianic deliverer who would assume the throne of David in accordance with the promise of 2 Sam. 7:4-17 (the Davidic covenant), thereby inaugurating a kingdom of perfection and righteousness that would last forever."[278] Matthew places more emphasis on this aspect of Jesus' identity than do the other evangelists.[279] For Matthew, the fact that the hopes of the Davidic Messiah come to rest in Jesus is the key element of his fulfillment motif. But he is not at all concerned that the line of descent is legal rather than genetic.[280] Indeed, this again points to divine action; God is also "able from these stones to raise up children to Abraham" (3:9).

Jesus is also "son of Abraham." Instead of stopping the genealogy at David, which could have implied that Jesus' Messiahship is an exclusively Jewish concern, the dual emphasis upon David and Abraham points to the fact that in Jesus, the Davidic Messiah, the promise of God to Abraham that through him all the families of the earth would be blessed (Gen 12:1-3), comes to fulfillment. That, in turn, confirms the wider connotation of the opening words (1:1: βίβλος γενέσεως), words that recall the opening of Genesis.[281] The story of Jesus, therefore, concerns the eschatological purposes of God. The purposes that God has had for His created order, flowing from the promise to Abraham, are now to be realized through Jesus Messiah. Here is Matthew's way of expressing "new creation" ideas.[282]

In what Kupp calls "the Christological pivot of the Gospel,"[283] Matthew describes the conception of Jesus through a citation of Isa. 7:14 (LXX).[284] The focus here is upon the name of the child. Once Joseph finds that Mary is pregnant, he is minded not to marry her.[285] But an angel appears to him in a dream to explain the situation. The angel also tells Joseph to name the child, thus "asserting his paternity and Jesus' legitimate place in his genealogy."[286] If the virginal conception in fulfillment of Isa. 7:14 were not enough, the fact that the name of the child is determined before birth indicates that His is not an accidental birth. Indeed, to this point everything that occurs is expressive of God's plan and purpose. "These heightened phenomena of God's presence in the now of the story are presented to the implied reader as a new era of divine immanence."[287]

The name "Jesus," given by the messenger, is further explained by the statement, "he will save his people from their sins" (Matt. 1:21). And it is for this reason that the people will come to call Him "Emmanuel."[288] The notion of salvation was widespread and clear enough. "Restoration eschatology," expressed in return from exile and new exodus metaphors, took on political, even violent, overtones in the minds of many. Although the gospel has clear political overtones for Matthew, every bit as much as it does for the other evangelists, in the aftermath of A.D. 66-70,[289] his readers, generally thought to be closer to Judaism than the implied readership of Luke, would certainly understand the risk of violence against the oppressors of God's people. Thus, Matthew emphasizes the internalization of God's purposes promised in the prophets by this phrase. Forgiveness of sins is a central feature of the new covenant relationship (see Jer. 31:31-34; Ezek. 36:25-28; cf. Isa. 1:16-17), which is being established through His coming and death. It is against this background that the phrase "from their sins" should be understood.[290]

The dominance of Old Testament motifs continues through chapter 2. Herod, the king of the Jews, is in fear of his throne. His inquiry of the Jerusalem scribes suggests that he knows he is a usurper, especially when he considers the portent of the star, clearly a sign from God. Herod is a symbol of the fact that the people of Israel are still in captivity, still awaiting deliverance.[291] His opposition to Jesus reaches appalling proportions, with "the massacre of the innocents."[292] Matthew again looks to the Scriptures to comment upon this event, perhaps after careful reflection on the whole of Jer. 31.[293] The new covenant motif that comes to clear expression in Jer. 31 is likely never far from Matthew's mind.

Magi from the east symbolize "the Gentiles who, unlike the Jews, prove receptive to the king and God's purposes in him. The realization of eschatological salvation means blessing for all the nations and not simply Israel—this in accord with God's promise to Abraham and the universalism of the prophets."[294] Their coming, too, fulfills Old Testament hopes when the nations shall stream to Zion (see Ps. 72:10-11; Isa. 60:3). The dominant motif in these two chapters, therefore, has been that Jesus, the Messiah, is God with us and that the eschatological hopes of Israel are about to be realized.

The two chapters also point in the direction of a "New Exodus/New Moses" concept, in what Allison calls "an infancy narrative permeated by Mosaic motifs."[295] This also helps us to understand the Sermon on the Mount. Notice that Jesus and His family escape to Egypt and that they return from Egypt following the death of Herod. Clearly, we have here a Jesus/Israel typology made explicit by the citation of Hos. 11:1 in which language originally referring to Israel now is applied to Jesus. This motif has also been present in the first chapter with a number of allusions to the birth of Moses. "We may say, then, that while Jesus culminates Israel's history in chapter 1, in chapter 2 he repeats it. Jesus is not only the last redeemer who is like the first redeemer, Moses, he is not only the messianic king who is like the great king David, but he is also like Israel in that he experiences exodus and exile and return."[296] To be sure, the return from exile is still to be completed, Jesus' identity with His people has yet to be confirmed, and the ultimate means of their salvation has yet to be accomplished. But Matthew has set his stall out with clarity and subtlety, reminding his readers that "in the history of Israel, God repeatedly brought salvation to his people, and he has now brought them to the time of fulfillment—eschatological fulfill-ment in one who relives, sums up, and brings to fruition all the history and experience of his people."[297]

## 1.2. The Baptism and Temptation Narratives

The identity and anointing of Jesus as the messianic servant and Son of God is certainly the central theme in the baptism nar-rative.[298] Clearly, this marks the transition between John and Je-sus, but Matthew has an important additional explanation of why Jesus should be baptized with John's baptism. No doubt there were those in the Early Church who found the paradox of the sinless One undergoing a baptism of repentance for the remis-sion of sins rather difficult. Matthew's explanation is threefold: he omits the statement in Mark 1:4, "a baptism of repentance for the forgiveness of sins"; he has John express great reluctance to baptize Jesus (Matt. 3:14); and he has Jesus explain: "it is proper for us in this way to fulfill all righteousness" (v. 15).

But what does this last statement mean? "Righteousness" is primarily a relational term in the Old Testament and need not be understood as moral goodness.[299] In this context, "righteousness" has nothing to do with Jesus' need to become moral or to submit to God's demand in one way or another. God's righteousness is an-other way of expressing His saving activity.[300] Hagner is surely on the right track when he states that "Jesus thereby shows his solidar-ity with his people in their need. The messiah is a representative person, the embodiment of Israel, whether as King or righteous Servant."[301] The righteousness He fulfills, therefore, is the full iden-tity with the people of God who are still in exile but are longing for God's action in history. He stands where His people stand, in the queue of people awaiting baptism in response to John's preaching, fully identifying with them in their hopes and needs. He is Emmanuel, God with us, who will save His people by fully identifying with them, thereby effecting God's deliverance. It natu-rally follows, then, that He should be endued with the Holy Spirit, confirmed as the beloved Son and embark upon His ministry.

When we come to the temptation narratives, the parallels be-tween Jesus and the people of God or the new Moses[302] are extensive. This is the testing of God's Son,[303] with reflection upon Deut. 6—8 shown in the Old Testament texts chosen to confront the tempter. Further identification with Israel is indicated. Jesus, the Son of God, is repeating the experience of Israel in the wilderness. This time, however, the Son is obedient and is able to continue with the ministry God has given Him just one episode earlier (3:16-17). Jesus confronts Satan, a reminder that opposition to God's good purposes is not confined to the Herods of this world. Rather, they are mere symptoms of the acquiescence of the created order in the rebellion against the Creator. All of the things upon which Jesus is tested can be interpreted as rightfully His: bread, security, and the rulership of this world. But each of them, in the hands of the tempter and in disobedience to God, becomes twisted. The desire for bread becomes an exercise of power for self-gratification; the desire for safety becomes the exercise of authority for self-aggrandizement; the easy way to the top of the world becomes a temptation to buy into the "big lie" that this world belongs to the devil. Jesus defeats the tempter at every point through the word of Scripture and in the power of the Spirit. Discipleship must also be expressed in full obedience to the Father's will, which is the only true indication of discipleship.

## 1.3. The Beginning of the Ministry

The geographical context and the content of Jesus' ministry are summarized in 4:12-17. For our purposes, two points are of importance. First, Jesus' ministry is set in the context of another Old Testament citation, again pointing to the fulfillment motif already seen to be prominent. Second, Jesus calls on His hearers to "Repent." A turn to God is required because Jesus is proclaiming the arrival of the Kingdom. A new covenantal relationship with God is being established: Jesus saves His people from their sins. Later in Matthew, Jesus is shown offering sinners a new beginning through belief in Him, welcoming them into intimate fellowship with himself. "The theme of 'salvation as pure gift' runs through the whole of Jesus' public proclamation."[304] At the same time, as Luz observes, "this imperative stands as the entry gate before the soon-to-come teaching concerning the higher righteousness which is to realised in the life of the Christian."[305]

There are enormous implications to such an announcement. In general terms, Israel believed that God's restoration of His people had not yet been accomplished as the prophets had promised. Equally strong was the conviction that God would act. Now He has acted. Davies and Allison suggest that the eschatological framework within which His action ought to be understood is that of Deutero-Isaiah. Like Isaiah, "The advent of God's kingdom did not, for Jesus, belong to a moment but constituted a series of events that would cover a period of time. . . . When Jesus announces that the kingdom of God has come and is coming, this means that the last act has begun but not yet reached its climax: the last things have come and will come."[306] But for Jesus, the emphasis lies on the radical belief that God has already acted.

Matthew also thinks of the fulfillment of God's purposes as extending to the Gentiles. Although there appear to be restrictions to the mission of Jesus in Matthew (see 10:6, for example), this is not to be understood as an exclusion of the Gentiles from the ultimate direction of Jesus' mission (see 28:16 ff.). Rather, Jesus is inviting the people of Israel to join Him in fulfilling God's good purposes, His rescue mission for the world. Jesus is God's Messiah who, through His teaching and actions, is offering God's salvation to all who would respond. As Meyer observes, "It is hardly possible to exaggerate the explosive power which this combination of 'gratuity' and 'present realization' gave to Jesus' proclamation."[307]

How, then, can we summarize what Matthew wants us to understand about Jesus in these first four chapters? The picture is one of a series of interlocking images and themes that all center around the motif of *fulfillment.* God's purposes come to their climax in Jesus, the prophet and teacher like Moses who teaches the word of God with authority. But He is at the same time the new Moses, leading the people on a new Exodus, out of exile, and establishing a new covenant.

Second, Jesus is *Emmanuel,* God with us. Jesus is not just another of the prophets or one of God's messengers. He is more, embodying in himself the promise of God's renewed presence among His people.

Third, He is *Jesus Messiah*. As Son of David, He inaugurates the longed-for return to the glorious reign of God. As Son of David, He is the Son of God who, like the king of old, represents His people. As His people's representative, He recapitulates the people's path from Egypt into the wilderness. But where Israel failed, Jesus succeeds. As Savior of His people, He offers them a new starting point in relation to God and to each other—the new covenant that, Matthew tells us later, is made possible through His death. But He is already establishing the new covenant community, calling disciples to himself and, as we are about to see, giving them His authoritative teaching.

These, then, are the words of the Messiah, Jesus, Son of God who teaches authoritatively because He is announcing the very word of God to His people. The Christological, ecclesiological, and eschatological contexts of the words is crucial for their understanding.[308] In sum, Jesus came "announcing and effecting the Kingdom of God in history"[309] and offering people a new relationship with the covenant God,[310] based entirely upon their relationship with Him as the representative of Israel and as God in their midst. And that is the decisive difference upon which all interpretations of His teaching hang.

## 2. THE SERMON ON THE MOUNT

As every first-year theology student knows, the Bible did not originally have chapter divisions. They were added later and, for the most part, are more helpful than detrimental. But just occasionally, the divisions get in the way of sound exegesis, leading readers of the text astray. This could well be an example. The chapter divisions here ignore a particularly important literary clue with the consequence that the Sermon on the Mount has been interpreted all too often as if the context we have just noted is irrelevant.

### 2.1. The Summary Statements

It is now a commonplace among students of the Sermon on the Mount that 4:23 forms an inclusio with 9:35. The summary in 4:23

describes Jesus' entire ministry: teaching, preaching, and healing. Initially, Jesus remains and works in Galilee, but His fame spreads throughout Syria. Indeed, by implication, Jesus' healings extended to those in Gentile Syria. The same summary is repeated in 9:35.

Matthew is particularly concerned with Jesus' teaching.[311] According to Kingsbury, while there are other preachers in Matthew, not so with teachers. Jesus is the only Teacher with authority who makes known "the will of God in terms of its original intention. . . . and when the exalted Son of God commissions his church to go to the nations, it is no accident that what these followers are given to 'teach' is 'all that *I* have commanded' (28:20)."[312] The Sermon on the Mount is "the heart of the Great Commission to teach to the Gentiles."[313]

It is difficult, however, to separate "teaching" from "preaching" the kingdom;[314] both are connected to Jesus' healing ministry. Word and deed go inextricably together, as is shown by the extent of Matthew's inclusio of 4:23 and 9:35—included within these brackets are the words and deeds of Jesus Messiah. But it is also important to see that the healing of Jesus is carried out whether or not belief in Him followed. These are actions of sheer compassion and thereby signs of the graciousness and good purposes of God's kingdom to all.[315] The holy God is merciful to His needy people. Jesus, Emmanuel, effects that mercy in His mission.

The teaching of Jesus begins with the Beatitudes, to which most attention is usually given. They certainly are important for understanding the range of Jesus' teaching here and in any holiness discussion, it is difficult to ignore 5:8, "Blessed are the pure in heart, for they will see God." Similarly, the blessing promised to those "who hunger and thirst for righteousness" (v. 6) is also important. But only a very brief account will be given to these verses here. Our main attention will be given to Jesus' discussion of the "greater righteousness" required of His disciples, before, at last, reaching 5:48.

## 2.2. Hungering and Thirsting After Righteousness

The concern that Matthew has for "righteousness" has already been noted.[316] Jesus is baptized to fulfill all righteousness, that is, to identify fully with His people in their need. It is not surprising, then, that Jesus announces this promise to His followers. The disciples of Jesus long for righteousness and are promised that they will be filled.

This is the fourth beatitude addressed to the oppressed, downtrodden, and the marginalized. They are those who are being called to be the new people of God.[317] Of course, each of these beatitudes has a spiritual dimension—it would be hard to explain Matthew's "blessed are the poor in spirit" (Matt. 5:3) compared to Luke's "blessed are you who are poor" (Luke 6:20) without considering Matthew's additional phrase—but to reduce them to an exclusively spiritual message distorts Matthew's meaning. If taken on its own, this fourth beatitude could be read as stating that those who hunger and thirst after righteousness will receive this gift from God when the Kingdom arrives in its fullness. On this reading, it is a spiritual gift for the future, and the hunger for righteousness shall be satisfied in a way that is quite similar to Paul's thinking in Romans: righteousness will be reckoned to His disciples as a gift of God's grace.

There is a clear gift character to the beatitude. This righteousness is not a human-generated quality of good living. Rather, it expresses "the dire need of a right relationship with God and others."[318] That renewed relationship is only possible through divine initiative. But righteousness as a spiritual gift to be received in the future cannot be Matthew's primary meaning.[319]

When the passage is read in the light of the rest of the Sermon on the Mount, there can be little doubt that Matthew understands righteousness in terms of demand as well as gift.[320] The use of the term elsewhere in the sermon is decisive for this perspective. According to 5:10, the disciples are blessed when persecuted for the sake of righteousness. Matthew does not mean they are persecuted because they are deemed to be righteous. This is lived righteousness, the "right conduct required by God."[321] They are blessed and persecuted in turn when they live the new life of the Kingdom.[322] They are called to active seeking after God's righteousness (see 6:33), the righteousness that is characteristic

of the kingdom of God. Thus, those who are hungering for righteousness are not merely looking for a future gift of acceptance
by God or of being counted as righteous.

Neither is this to be understood primarily in individual terms.
Matthew is not speaking here only about a right relationship with
God. For some commentators, this sits uncomfortably with what
they see as Paul's emphasis on the God who justifies the ungodly.[323] But Matthew is not speaking primarily of the longing of an individual to be put into a right relationship with God. To be sure,
being filled with God's righteousness depends upon being in a
right relationship with God. As Bruner notes, "A righteousness separated from one's relationship with God is unknown to Jewish
piety."[324] But the crucial point is this. Righteousness has a social
context. This is the characteristic of the new people of God now
because Jesus is bringing in the new covenant relationship with
His people. This is demand as well as gift. The hunger is for
justice,[325] for right relationships in community and, as Matthew
notes later, even with enemies (5:45-48). Bruner reminds us, "Matthew's Jesus will unforgettably hammer away at this prophetic requirement of personal and social righteousness in text after text."[326]

There is, of course, a future eschatological dimension to all
of this. Bruner argues that the danger in interpreting this passage
is making it "insufficiently eschatological"[327] because a focus on
the present may lead to a narrow view of righteousness confined
to the personal and spiritual. But the danger of interpreting only
in future terms is equally problematic. The notion that "righteousness . . . must ever be sought . . . and always be the goal
which lies ahead: it is never in the grasp"[328] misses the point that
the Kingdom has already arrived in the person and work of Jesus
Messiah in anticipation of its future consummation. Righteousness in the kingdom of God is dynamic and relational and is to
be reflected in the way that the community lives in the community itself and before the world. This is both the character and
goal for those who are the people of God, the "greater righteousness" demanded in 5:21.[329]

While the consummation of righteousness in all of God's

created order is clearly the goal of Matthew's teaching (see 6:10), the emphasis upon righteous conduct in the community and toward the world is a demand that is relevant for the community of faith now. The righteousness that the disciples long for "expresses the new relationship that one has with God and with others in view of Jesus' ministry; it expresses the commensurate conduct growing out of this relationship and demanded by Jesus. Such relationship and such conduct are characteristic of the age of salvation and are part of Jesus' coming as the fulfilment of the Old Testament promise, the Messiah Son of God who comes declaring and effecting the Kingdom present and future."[330]

## 2.3. The Pure in Heart

The blessed ones in this beatitude are those who are pure in heart. Two concerns arise in this discussion. First, what does it mean to be "pure of heart"?

In biblical thought, the heart is the center of the will and emotions—the mainspring of all action. It really refers to people at the core of their being. It is biblical commonplace that while humans look on the outward appearance, God knows the heart, what a person is in the inner being.[331] Interestingly enough, none of the Beatitudes offers advice on specific conduct.

The language itself probably reflects Ps. 24 where true worshipers of God approach His holy hill with clean hands and pure hearts. Matthew does not take up the notion of clean hands probably because Jesus was concerned with the true definition of purity. Holiness, in the view of Jesus, was not maintained by ritual purity—clean hands—but by the integrity of being that identified wholly and unreservedly with the purposes of God in compassion and redemption for His lost and dying world. That kind of oneness with God's purposes issued in behavior that was consistent. To have a pure heart in the view of Jesus was to have that single-minded devotion to God that centered on His purposes for His created order. It was an invitation to imitate God.[332] The bitter criticisms by the Matthean Jesus against His fellow holiness people, the Pharisees, was that their inner core did not match their outward piety (see especially Matt. 23). Again and again, Jesus returns to the theme of the integrity of the whole being. In sum, purity of heart is the undivided heart, people of integrity.[333]

The second question centers upon when the pure in heart see God. Most commentators see the vision of God as pointing firmly to the future, that is, the consummation of all things.[334] But while this is certainly the ultimate direction of the beatitude, like the others it also has a present reality. Those who know Jesus and have seen that He is Emmanuel, God with us, also see Jesus announcing and inaugurating the kingdom of God. Hence, the notion of a pure heart and of seeing God has both future and present fulfillments. Purity of heart, that single-minded devotion to God that aligns the human will with that of the Father, is made possible in relationship with Jesus Messiah. "The power for purity of heart is supplied by the in-breaking kingdom that comes through the im-press [*sic*] of Jesus' words. But the will thus mobilized can and will grasp the power given."[335]

This, then, is language for now and the future. Single-minded devotion to God in which the center of one's being is wholeheartedly devoted to Him through the power of the Kingdom is the gift and demand of God.[336]

## 2.4. The Greater Righteousness

"For I tell you, unless your righteousness exceeds that of the scribes and Pharisees, you will never enter the kingdom of heaven" (5:20). So says Jesus solemnly to all of His disciples. And this is just after He has, with equal solemnity, told them that "until heaven and earth pass away, not one letter, not one stroke of a letter, will pass from the law until all is accomplished" (v. 18).

These verses form a *crux interpretatum* in Matthew. Taken from its historical and literary context, this pericope appears to suggest that Jesus considers all the Torah to be binding on the new people of God. Indeed, it might be argued that Jesus is here promulgating a more rigorous adherence to the legal requirements of the Law than even the Pharisees are expecting. On this view, Jesus' words are a prescription for lifelong duty that will ultimately lead to entrance into the kingdom of God. Or, to put it another way, the kind of holiness Jesus is demanding of His disciples is ever more strict and rigorous adherence to a legal code. Holiness then becomes an achievement of performance targets set out by Jesus.[337] This, in itself, would not be surprising because, as McKnight reminds us, the radical pursuit of holiness was one option in second Temple Judaism.[338] The Matthean Jesus, then, is the classical Christian exponent of a non-Pauline "works righteousness."[339] Indeed, Keener believes that "Jesus essentially warns prospective followers, 'My demands are more stringent than other interpretations of the law.' . . . Jesus makes the law more stringent in this passage, not less."[340] But does that analysis stand careful scrutiny?[341]

Once again, the proper understanding of these words here can only be gained through understanding the bigger picture, what Meyer calls "a totality of meaning."[342] Much of that work has already been done in this chapter. Two further points need to be noted, however. This is a call to all of His disciples by Jesus Messiah. There is no hint whatsoever that the Sermon on the Mount is addressed to a select group of disciples. Although Matt. 5:1 notes that "when Jesus saw the crowds, he went up the mountain; and after he sat down, *his disciples* came to him" (italics added), the conclusion to the section in 7:28-29 reads, "Now when Jesus had finished saying these things, *the crowds were astounded* at his teaching, for he taught them as one having authority, and not as their scribes" (italics added). Taken together, it is clear that Matthew does not want the Sermon on the Mount to be read as exclusive teaching to an inner group of disciples but as teaching to all who wish to come to Him to be His disciples. It is invitation as well as command. Second, the Matthean Jesus has already announced that God is acting *now* to bring His Torah promises, including the hope for a new covenant, to fulfillment, not in some distant future. The Kingdom is being inaugurated in His ministry now, and He would bring it to consummation. Already in the Beatitudes and the verses immediately before 5:17, the subversive nature of the Kingdom and its membership can be seen: first are last; sinners are invited to enter ahead of the righteous; the Kingdom is coming, not through violent revolution, but through the person of Jesus. The new people of God are con-stituted simply through belief in Him, not the conventional means of repentance and restoration.

With this in mind, we can now address the questions this passage raises. First, in what sense does Jesus come to fulfill the Law and the Prophets? A variety of answers has been given but, on balance, the best answer is to see this in terms of bringing the Law and the Prophets to their intended purpose. Hagner argues that "this is the law as understood in the context of the fulfill-ment of God's purposes announced by Jesus. For Jesus is the goal of the law and prophets."[343] This point needs further develop-ment, however. Keener is quite right to remind us that "the king-dom grace Jesus proclaimed was not the workless grace of much of Western Christianity; in the Gospels the kingdom message *transforms* those who meekly embrace it, just as it crushes the ar-rogant, the religiously and socially satisfied."[344] But neither is it salvation by works. Such a perspective was not part of authentic second Temple Judaism, and Jesus is not teaching it here.[345]

Matthew has already demonstrated by his careful and exten-sive use of Scripture the way in which he wishes this statement to be read. It is this: Jesus is the ultimate fulfillment of God's prom-ised salvation in history, "the one who brings the new relationship between God and humankind promised in the Scriptures."[346] The continuity with the Scriptures remains, of course. Hagner con-cludes that Jesus is the "bringer of the kingdom, and hence the fi-nal interpreter of the law's meaning. The law as *he* teaches it is valid for all time, and thus in effect the law is upheld."[347]

In that last analysis, if Jesus is indeed making "the law more stringent,"[348] He merely exchanges one potential legalism for an-other. And the problem with any form of legalism, be it based up-on Mosaic or any other Torah, in addition to its burdensome char-acter, is its inability to create the conditions under which it is fulfilled and to respond to changing situations. Is this, then, what Matthew intends? The answer to that question must be held in abeyance for a moment while we consider the rest of this passage.

The second question is this: What are we to make of the

next two verses that seem to suggest that even the minutiae of the Law have eternal validity? Here we come to a more difficult discussion, because this centers on the phrase "until heaven and earth pass away." In other words, all of the small parts of the Law have eternal validity, a literalistic reading that has led to a number of tragic consequences.[349] Selected parts of Jesus' own teaching in Matt. 5:22-48 have been taken very rigidly while other parts have been understood to be the figures of speech that they undoubtedly are.[350] More generally, scholars interpret this to mean that "the scriptural authority of the Torah will not pass away as long as the conditions of the transitory would persist," and therefore these words point to the end of history itself.[351] As Betz admits, such a conclusion places Matthew's discussion in potential conflict with Paul's view (see Gal. 3:19-25; Rom. 10:4).[352] But is this conclusion necessary?

Perhaps a way forward might be found through a closer look at the structure of the verse. The crucial phrases in 5:18—"until heaven and earth pass away" and "until all is accomplished"— are set in chiastic parallelism as follows:

A    Until heaven and earth pass away,

    B    Not one letter, not one stroke of a letter,

    B1  Will pass from the law

A1  Until all is accomplished.

This parallelism suggests that phrases A and A1 are making a similar point. Or, to put it another way, it is possible that "until heaven and earth pass away" should be understood in light of "until all is accomplished" rather than the other way around. If this is so, then it is important to try to understand how Matthew understands the phrase "until all is accomplished." Three interpretations are possible: (1) the end of the world, (2) until the requirements of the Law are kept, (3) until that to which it points is fulfilled.[353] When Matthew uses very similar language in 24:34, he prefaces the remark by having Jesus say, "This generation will not pass away until all these things have taken place." In that passage, the best interpretation of the phrase "this generation will not pass away" strongly suggests that Jesus is there talking about the fall of Jerusalem in

A.D. 66-70. It follows that the meaning of "until all is accomplished" in 5:18 is likely the third option.

An interesting further support to this view comes from an alternative meaning of "heaven and earth" suggested by Crispin Fletcher-Louis. Fletcher-Louis has argued that "the passing away of heaven and earth [is] a specifically Christologically focused event within imminent history."[354] In fact, the phrase "heaven and earth" could actually refer to the Temple itself in the mythology of second Temple Judaism. That would explain, therefore, why Matthew uses the phrase "until all is accomplished" as the parallel to "until heaven and earth pass away": he sees the "cross and resurrection . . . [as the] decisive moment at which heaven and earth passed away (and were recreated at the resurrection)."[355] On this reading the minutiae of the Law are relativized because they are clearly temporary until the death and resurrection of Jesus.[356] Keeping the Law in its detail is no longer the path to holiness, if it ever was.

But what about the final verse? It seems to be quantitative in meaning: "except your righteousness exceeds that of the scribes and Pharisees"—a greater quantity of righteousness.[357] Immediately following 5:17-20, the Matthean Jesus elaborates on the theme of the greater righteousness expected of the new people of God. Here we return to our earlier question. Does this make Jesus the new Moses promulgating a new law with ever more stringent legal requirements as entry criteria to the Kingdom? According to Allison, "Jesus is the Moses-like Messiah who proclaims the eschatological will of God on a mountain typologically equated with Sinai."[358]

Allison's arguments are impressive. Much of the first two chapters of Matthew is evocative of the Moses/Sinai traditions. At first glance the five (or six) so-called antitheses in 5:21-48 might appear to suggest that Jesus is indeed acting as a new Moses and giving a new Torah. Taken on their own, they seem to be a new Torah.[359] Indeed, to the extent that Jesus is reinterpreting the Torah in light of the new situation, he is a Moses-like figure. To be sure, this is "eschatological Torah, perhaps in accord with Jeremiah 31, interpreted as foretelling an internalisation of the Mosaic law."[360]

But to suggest that Jesus' teaching is a new law *tout simple* is unlikely. In His "You have heard that it said, . . . but I say to you" form of address, Jesus speaks with even greater authority than Moses, an authority based on His vocation not only as the proclaimer of the kingdom of God but as its embodiment. As Luz observes, "God's will, as proclaimed in the Sermon on the Mount, is not simply an abstract command; it is the command of that same God who accompanies his people in the form of Jesus."[361] In the memorable words of Guelich, "Jesus came bringing not a new law but a new covenant. . . . God offers to his own a new starting point in relationship with himself and with others."[362] Hence, in Matt. 5:21-48, Jesus is not simply adding ever more restrictive legal boundaries. Rather, He is pointing to the weakness of all approaches to the Torah legally construed by showing, through the sharp hyperbole of some of the antitheses, the impossibility of fulfilling the Law conceived as an external.

None of this could be construed as contrary to the Law and the Prophets. Rather, as Wright notes, Jesus' claim is that

> it is his interpretation of the vocation and destiny of Israel that is in ultimate continuity with the Torah and the Prophets, and the scribes and Pharisees have got it wrong. The kingdom will not override Moses and the Prophets . . . but Israel must not remain content with the shallow reading of scripture that uses it merely to bolster her own national security. There is a deeper meaning in the sacred writings than first-century Israel had grasped: it is this deeper meaning that Jesus is commending.[363]

Our answer to the key question, "Is Jesus proclaiming a new, more stringent legal code?" depends upon Guelich's insight. Jesus came proclaiming a new covenant, not a new law. But implicit in covenant is always the response of obedience to the grace offered in the covenant. Jesus is neither legalistic nor antinomian. Jesus' Torah intensification implies that mere compliance with the Torah is not adequate because that does not really reflect the intentions of the Lawgiver. Matthew thinks that this moves beyond a rabbinical debate between equal authorities because Jesus is the unique authority, Emmanuel and Messiah. In Matthew's view, Jesus came offering people a new relationship with the covenant God and each other,[364] based entirely upon their relationship with Him as the representative of Israel and as God in their midst.

To put it another way, Jesus doesn't simply intensify the Torah; He radicalizes it by returning again and again to first principles and, hence, to a renewed emphasis on its inner purpose. As Ben Meyer observes, "The Torah would be thereby surpassed, indeed, but only in its own direction. The inner dynamism of Torah had always been the honour of God and one's parents and the rights of one's neighbour. Now this inner dynamism would not be transcended but realized; only the Torah's external forms and limits would be transcended and rendered obsolete."[365] Jesus' followers, then, would keep the Torah, but "only to the extent that it expressed conduct in keeping with the Father's will as revealed through Jesus Messiah."[366] Here was the key. His attitude was rather liberal with respect to some of the ritual demands of the Law. The Torah was not ultimate; insofar as the Torah pointed beyond itself to the coming kingdom of God, it was provisional in the light of the Kingdom's arrival. Of course, "it is not a question of two different laws, but of one reality—the will of God—witnessed to by the law and the prophets, but now made plain by Jesus."[367]

Jesus is bringing to fulfillment those promises of a new covenant (see Jer. 36:36 ff.; Ezek. 31:26 ff.) in which the Law becomes part of the interiority of the covenanted people, not an external code. This new law on the heart, the circumcision of the heart (see Rom. 2:29), is based on the new relationship that Matthew later tells us is brought to fruition by the death of Jesus Messiah. The demands are no longer demands. They are the response made possible because of the new starting point, a completely new relationship between God and His people; it is also a new starting point for human relationships, based on forgiveness and reconciliation. That is the context of the following "antitheses" in 5:21-48.

## 2.5. Perfect like Your Father

We come, finally, to our critical verse. In many ways, the hard work has already been done because we have already established that this is not a new legal requirement, nor is it an entrance test to the Kingdom. Positively, we have already shown that Jesus' identity is the basis for a correct understanding of His teaching. We also know that this teaching is directed to all disciples, those who are already proleptically part of His new covenant community, not a general aphorism for nice people.

The problem in this verse comes from understanding the word "perfect." We immediately think of *flawless* when we think of perfect, and we know that it is impossible to be flawless like God the Father. How can we solve this problem?

A useful starting point might be to look at the Old Testament use of the terms usually translated τέλειος in the New Testament. According to Gen. 17:1, Abraham was called to respond to the promise of God and to walk blamelessly before God. Clearly, this was not a flawless performance. (Remember Abraham's "she's my sister" story to Pharaoh [12:11-20] and again to Abimelech [chap. 20] about his wife, Sarah?) Rather, Abraham was called to walk in obedience and faith, putting his trust in God's call. Here is no static flawlessness but a dynamic, ongoing relationship. We can, therefore, safely set aside the "flawless" definition of "perfect" with respect to humans.

Matthew uses the term τέλειος in another important passage as well. In 19:16-21, the crucial parts of the narrative read: "Then someone came to him and said, 'Teacher, what good must I do to inherit eternal life?'" Jesus answered, "'If you wish to enter into life, keep the commandments.' . . . The young man said to him, 'I have kept all these [commandments]; what do I still lack?' Jesus said to him, 'If you wish to be perfect [Εἰ θέλεις τέλειος εἶναι], go, sell your possessions, and give the money to the poor, and you will have treasure in heaven; then come, follow me.'" At first glance, this story might seem to imply that all may "enter into life" (v. 17) by keeping the commandments, but others are to go on to a higher level of spiritual life by being "perfect,"[368] perhaps on the lines of entry into the Qumran community.[369] But the rest of the pericope does not support this view of a two-tiered discipleship. This young man turns away from Jesus when faced with the cost of discipleship. As France notes, "The demands of discipleship will vary for different individuals and situations. But they will never be less than total availability to the claims of Jesus, however differently these apply in practice."[370] This is, rather, "the radicalizing of the moral demand in xix.17."[371]

We have already noted that the teaching in the Sermon on the Mount is not just for a select inner circle of disciples, a point drawn out by Gerhard Barth.[372] He argues that "perfection is the decisive characteristic of the new community . . . [and] is demanded of the whole community."[373] Matt. 5:48 cannot, therefore, refer to a higher level of achievement required of some disciples. Nor is it an isolated perfection apart from the community. *"All* disciples are called to the 'greater righteousness' of 5:20, and to be 'perfect' (5:48)."[374]

Perhaps even more important, however, is the point established above: Jesus believed himself to be God's spokesperson, the One to whom the Law and Prophets pointed, the authoritative and unprecedented interpreter of the Law as God's purpose.

Later in the Gospel, Matthew makes explicit what has already been implicit in our interpretation of 5:17-20. According to 22:36-40, Jesus is asked, "'Teacher, which commandment in the law is the greatest?'" And Jesus said to him, "'You shall love the Lord your God with all your heart, and with all your soul, and with all your mind. This is the greatest and the first commandment. And a second is like it, 'You shall love your neighbor as yourself.' On these two commandments hang all the law and the prophets." Here, now, we discover what it means to fulfill the inner dynamic of the Law and the Prophets as well as the meaning of the greater righteousness.

Jesus' combination of these two commands is distinctive. As Keener notes, "In the multiplicity of other proposals concerning the greatest commandment in antiquity, only Jesus wielded the moral authority among His followers to focus their ethics so profoundly around a single theme."[375] Jesus considered love to be the center of the Law, which was the whole of the Torah in its divine intention. Anything that interfered with fulfilling the inner intention of the Law was mere legalism.

Is this, then, the most rigorous application of the Law? If so, it is a legalistic impossibility. But if the demand is based on the new covenant relationship, it comes from the gift of God's righteousness, His holiness. It is not a consequence of greater effort; it is the result of God's gift of the new heart. In fact, the greater righteousness of 5:20 turns out to be nothing less than being perfect like our Father. We are to act like Him in our lives. Our lives, the lives of God's holy people, filled with God's grace, are to mirror that grace in our relationships with all. Those who have been called to be disciples by Jesus Messiah have been brought into a new covenant relationship with God and neighbor by which they are enabled to live lives that reflect the reality of the new situation.

The demand is not a new and more exacting law but rather the fruit of the new relationships already established in Christ— new God/human and human/human relationships. In this context, then, "perfect" is not a moral, legal standard at all. Rather, it points to wholeheartedness, complete devotion. Its primary orientation is toward the community. The new people of God are to live like their Father in all of their relationships at all times—even in relationship to enemies. It is in this sense that John Wesley's "perfect in love" captures the essence of this demand. For Matthew, "the love commandment stands at the center"[376] of the whole Sermon on the Mount. To be perfect like your Father is to have that perfect love, that single-minded devotion to God and love of neighbor that is the summation and fulfillment of God's great commands to us.

Is it realizable now? Yes, it is, according to the Matthean Jesus. This is a present reality for the new people of God because disciples are called to a totally God-centered and neighbor-centered mind-set. They have entered into that relationship with their

Father in which they are enabled to model His love, mercy, and justice to their neighbors. But it also remains a future hope because disciples live in this evil age, in fallen flesh and in solidarity with the rest of unredeemed humanity. If this is a performance target, it cannot be reached. Performance often falls short of flawlessness, and disciples require the forgiveness of sins available in the new covenant relationship. It is not by accident that the Lord's Prayer, with its petition for forgiveness, follows soon after.

## 3. Aspects of Holiness in Matthew

Who, then, is this person who calls disciples to be perfect like their Father? And what does it mean? The answer of the second question depends upon the first. Jesus is the One who calls the disciples. He brings God's good purposes to their climax, teaching with authority, leading the people on a new Exodus, and establishing a new covenant written on the heart. Because He is *Emmanuel* and *Messiah,* He inaugurates the glorious reign of God. As His people's Savior and representative, He offers them a new starting point in relation to God and to each other— the new covenant that, Matthew tells us later, is made possible through His death.

These, then, are the words of the Messiah, Jesus, Son of God, who teaches authoritatively because He is announcing the very word of God to His people. In sum, Jesus is proclaiming the kingdom of God in history and offering people a new relationship with the covenant God and within the community, based entirely upon their relationship with Him as the representative of Israel and as God in their midst. And that makes all the difference.

In fact, the greater righteousness of 5:20 turns out to be nothing less than being perfect like our Father. Jesus considers love to be the center of the Law because it sums up the whole of the Torah in its divine intention. Anything that interferes with fulfilling the inner intention of the Law is mere legalism. Single-minded devotion to God and love of neighbor, flowing from the people of God in loving relationship with the holy God through Jesus Messiah by the Spirit, is the motivational center of Christian holiness.

# 6

# HOLINESS AND THE GOSPELS
## LESSONS IN THE HOLY LIFE

◆

The theological journey through the four Gospels is finished. But this has not been an attempt to articulate a theology of the Gospels. Our purpose has been rather more modest. We have been looking for clues that might enhance our understanding of Christian holiness through paying attention to the story of Jesus and His disciples. Whatever gains there have been probably match the modesty of purpose. After all, the stories are well known. And yet, they may challenge us as well. Perhaps the most important lessons we have learned can be summed up in a few brief comments on some themes.

## 1. CHRISTIAN HOLINESS IS CENTERED IN THE TRIUNE GOD

All of the Gospels have an implicit Trinitarian understanding of God. It may not have the sophistication of later developments by the Greek Fathers, but their rudimentary understanding of who God is is the foundation for Christian holiness. The loving and lively Being-in-Communion that is holy Trinity undergirds God's relationship with the created order, the origin of God's perpetual sustaining and rescue mission, and the model for Christian holy living.

The implications of this for Christian holiness are profound. Humans have been created in the image of God but have an estranged relationship with their Creator. Salvation may be described as being brought back into that quality of relationship that God intends. Through the salvation offered by the triune God, the loving relationship with the holy God is restored. People are invited to participate in the mutual love that is the energizing force of the Trinity. That is not to say that creatures lose their creatureliness. Christians always remain created creatures of God who participate in the life of God, rather than being absorbed into the being of God.

This energizing love of the holy Trinity becomes the key identifying characteristic of the people of God as they live in communion with God and their neighbors. Any understanding of the people of God, of love to our neighbors, and of our mission to the world is based upon who God is and the life of the holy Trinity. In living lives indwelt by the Spirit and in communion with God through the Spirit, God's people reflect God's image as loving relational beings in harmony with the rest of the created order. Christian love and unity have their source in the love and unity of the holy Trinity. The life of the people of God, then, is utterly dependent upon the source of all life. Christian holiness and the sanctification of God's people are all part of the mutuality and indwelling of Christians in the holy Trinity.

The Gospels, of course, all focus upon the Incarnate One. All of them affirm that God in the person of Jesus enters into the human condition, taking on our fallen flesh. In so doing, He offers a new starting point for humankind by His perfect obedience to the Father. This obedience is offered, not by exercising His divine prerogatives, but within the context of the genealogy of all other sons and daughters of Adam. He lives His human life from beginning to end in and through the Spirit and makes real decisions in our real world, all in the power of the Spirit. He sets a pattern for His disciples, showing that Christian holiness is possible when lives are lived in relationship with God through the power of the Holy Spirit.

The fact that Jesus is also the Holy One of God means that God is with His people. Whether it is as "Emmanuel, God with us," or as "the Beloved Son," Jesus is pictured as the Holy One in the midst of His people, the locale of God among His people. Not only is He conceived of the Spirit and bears the Spirit, but as the Beloved Son He is the giver of the Spirit as well. Thus, those who are gathered around Jesus are God's holy people. Their holiness is a derived holiness based on their relationship to the Holy One. It is never a performance-based holiness, in sharp contrast to all of the other holiness movements of the day.

## 2. CHRISTIAN HOLINESS IS DEFINED BY JESUS

The redefinition of holiness is probably the most important lesson learned from the Gospels. In bluntest terms, Jesus calls into question the whole connection between holiness and separation. In doing so, Jesus returns the conception of holiness to its source in the very being of God. The result is that holiness is no longer to be misconstrued as separation from neighbor but is to be expressed as love of neighbor. For most of the other holiness movements of the day, separation had become an end in itself because that was thought to be the way to achieve and maintain the purity required by the holy God. But Jesus shows that when separateness becomes the prime identity marker of the people, their attempt to preserve holiness becomes a barrier to engaging with God in His mission in the world.

For Jesus, holiness is contagious, outgoing, embracing, and joyous. It transforms and brings reconciliation. It extends compassion to the marginalized so that they are brought into the circle of those who do the will of God. This holiness is a dynamic power emanating from the source of holiness, the Holy One. It is stronger than any acquired impurity. Time and again the compassion of Jesus for those who are the marginalized overrides the legitimate concern for purity.

This does not mean that God's holy people no longer are concerned with holy living. On the contrary. Holy living is the fruit of the new covenant relationship being established in Christ —new God/human and human/human relationships. In that new relationship, disciples are called to be perfect like our Father. Jesus' ethical teaching is an intensification of holiness, but only in the direction of God's original intention. The purity of God's holy people is really an inner matter that issues in ethical living. Discipleship is expressed in full obedience to the Father's will, that greater righteousness, which is the only true indication of discipleship. But this has nothing to do with a moral, legal standard and everything to do with reflecting the compassionate, merciful being of the Heavenly Father. Legalism doesn't work because it looks only at external performance targets.

Through His words and deeds, Jesus reveals the heart of God. Although His opponents should know better, they have forgotten that God is not a tyrannical vigilante but a gracious and loving God who is slow to anger and plenteous in mercy. So His opponents would rather continue to be God's holy people their own way—keeping pure from contamination, defending God's holiness against the foreigners, the tax collectors, the prostitutes and sinners, keeping their theological categories clear.

### 3. Christian Holiness Is Communal and Personal

Jesus renews God's call to Israel but with a difference. Specifically, He calls Twelve apostles to represent the whole people of God. They are now the vanguard of the kingdom of priests and holy nation that God is re-creating. Then He gathers around himself a representative collection of those on the fringes of society. Instead of being outside the boundaries of God's purposes, the marginalized (including Gentiles) are the objects of divine grace. That is not a readily accepted recasting of God's purposes, but Jesus challenges His opponents to celebrate the fulfillment of God's bigger purposes in this community-without-walls and to welcome them into its intimate fellowship.

The Gospels picture individuals responding to Jesus' invitation, but this is always an invitation to join a people. Discipleship is never an individual calling. Nor are disciples the focal point; Jesus is. Therefore, disciples do not determine the parameters of the people of God. Rather, the determining criterion for discipleship is simply being part of His people, in relationship to Jesus, the Holy One of God. Christian holiness is thus a social, not an individual, phenomenon.

The essence of the life of this community is love made possible through the indwelling of the Spirit. It is expressed in participation in the loving life of the community and in the loving mission of God to the world. This kind of love is the whole of the Torah in its divine intention and the fulfillment of all God's purposes.

By responding to the call to join the new people of God, disciples are transformed by being in relationship with the Holy One. They are sanctified in this relationship to Jesus who himself has been sanctified for God's mission, that is, set apart and sent on this mission.

## 4. Christian Holiness Is a Journey

This may seem to be an obvious point, but the stories about the disciples can challenge us to rethink our understanding of Christian holiness. The disciples embark on a journey with the Holy One of God. Although the Gospels are rather less prescriptive about the nature of the starting point than some might wish, they are adamant that the journey with Jesus must begin. In this journey wholehearted allegiance to Him is required. Halfhearted discipleship is never an option, nor are there different classes of discipleship. Rather, this open-ended journey demands all and is for all who would follow.

The Gospels, however, never lose touch with reality. They know that the journey is long and riddled with potential pitfalls. They also are frank about the fact that even the most committed of disciples may fail. And they are equally clear that forgiveness and restoration are offered to failed disciples.

## 5. Christian Holiness Is Present Life and Future Goal

Jesus claims that God's good purposes are now coming to their fulfillment in His words and deeds. The story of Jesus, therefore, concerns the purposes that God has always had. They are now being realized. The time for the new in-the-heart Torah promised by the Prophets has arrived. In some ways, the nowness of the Good News gives urgency to the mission and message of Jesus.

It is also a future hope. The realism of the Gospels about the present age tempers any triumphalism. Although disciples are safe close to the Holy One, they still live in this evil age, still in fallen flesh, and still in solidarity with the rest of unredeemed humanity. Disciples live and share in this nexus of relationships that is based on the domination system. Because they are in solidarity with the rest of humanity in this system, they are caught in the tension between "the already" and "the not yet." Triumph indeed is promised, but the "not yet" of the disciples, together with that of the groaning creation, awaits the ultimate triumph of God. But that does not call for an abandonment of the world to its fate. On the contrary, disciples are called to participate in God's rescue mission so that they, too, will finally be part of that final restoration by God.

## 6. So What?

"So what?" This short discussion on aspects of holiness in the Gospels has suggested a few interesting points about Christian holiness. But are there lessons to be learned? Perhaps. At least a series of questions needs to be asked.

- Does the connection between holiness and separation need to be challenged?
- Does a concern for holy living vitiate our willingness to be involved with the marginalized in compassion?
- Have we become so concerned with the starting point that we've neglected the journey?
- Have we really understood that failure is possible on the journey and that forgiveness and restoration are possible?
- Do we try to live a holy life through our own effort and, when that fails, dismiss the whole notion of holy living?
- Have we somehow forgotten about the effectiveness of the indwelling Spirit in persons and the community of faith as the sole source of our effectiveness in mission and obedience?
- Do we really believe that God is Trinity and invites us into the very loving life of the Trinity?
- Do we settle for a unity "from below" and mistake sentimentality for koinonia?

- Have we succumbed to the individualism of our society to such an extent that we cannot conceive of our mutuality with each other, never mind the triune God?
- Have we forgotten the simple truth that Christian holiness is nothing more nor less than single-minded and whole-hearted love of God and neighbor?

In sum, the Gospels may have a great deal more to say about Christian holiness than we might have imagined. But they only represent an aspect of New Testament theology. Christian theology, especially in its Protestant guise, has usually turned to Paul for its foundation. Not surprisingly, Paul's voice has been highly influential in our understanding of Christian holiness. But the evangelists have a story to tell and a contribution to make. It can only be hoped that this brief discussion will have encouraged us to bring their contribution to the discussion as well.

It may be that we need to listen again to Paul as well, but that's another story.

*Sola gloria deo*

# NOTES

1. See Keith Drury, for example, in an address to the Christian Holiness Association Presidential Breakfast titled "The Holiness Movement Is Dead," available at http://www.indwes.edu/tuesday/menu.htm.

2. See Mark R. Quanstrom, *A Century of Holiness Theology: The Doctrine of Entire Sanctification in the Church of the Nazarene: From Extravagant Hope to Limited Expectation* (Kansas City: Nazarene Publishing House, 2004).

3. See Mildred Bangs Wynkoop, *A Theology of Love: The Dynamic of Wesleyanism* (Kansas City: Beacon Hill Press of Kansas City, 1972), chap. 3, "The Credibility Gap."

4. To our surprise, our postgraduate M.A. in theology (Aspects of Christian Holiness) has attracted more candidates from outside the Holiness tradition than from within.

5. The roots of Pentecostalism and the charismatic movement are deep in the same soil as those of the Holiness Movement. Although the parting of the ways between the two was acrimonious, there are some encouraging signs of rapprochement between these two close relatives.

6. See, for example, Robert E. Webber, *Evangelicals on the Canterbury Trail* (London: Moorhouse, 1989).

7. See the discussions of the intersection of Wesleyan theology with Orthodoxy in recent issues of the *Wesleyan Theological Journal*

8. See, for example, Miroslav Volf, *After Our Likeness: The Church as the Image of the Trinity,* Sacra Doctrina (Grand Rapids/Cambridge: Eerdmans, 1998) and the very helpful introduction by Timothy Ware (Bishop Kallistos of Diokleia), *The Orthodox Church,* rev. ed. (London: Penguin, 1993).

9. See Richard Bauckham and Trevor Hart, *Hope Against Hope: Christian Eschatology in Contemporary Context* (London: DLT, 1999), who document the bankruptcy in theology that came from too close an identification with modernity and a trenchant warning against aligning theology to any postmodern agenda.

10. Recent statistics suggest that there are close to 380 million Pentecostal/charismatic renewal adherents worldwide, but they are underrepresented in higher education.

11. The launching of the *Journal of Pentecostal Theology* (JPT) in 1990 is a major step in this direction. See Mark W. G. Stibbe, "The Theology of Renewal and the Renewal of Theology," JPT 3 (1993), 71-90, for a bibliography of scholarly work coming from the charismatic renewal movement between 1983 and 1993. A recent important example is the work of Clark D. Pinnock, *The Flame of Love* (Downers Grove, Ill.: InterVarsity Press, 1998) and the careful reviews of his work in the JPT.

12. See T. A. Noble, "1988 Collins Holiness Lectures" (unpublished lectures delivered at Canadian Nazarene College, Winnipeg, Manitoba), for a serious attempt to integrate the Wesleyan understanding of Christian holiness with the doctrines of Christology, Atonement, and Trinity.

13. See the "Re-Minting Christian Holiness" articles on http://holiness.nazarene.ac.uk/ and the recent book by Samuel M. Powell, *Holiness in the 21st Century: Call, Consecration, and Obedience Perfected in Love* (San Diego: Point Loma Press, 2004).

14. W. T. Purkiser, *Exploring Christian Holiness*. Vol. 1, *Biblical Foundations* (Kansas City: Beacon Hill Press of Kansas City, 1983), 19.

15. John E. Hartley, *Leviticus,* vol. 4 of *Word Biblical Commentary* (WBC) (Dallas: Word, 1992), lvi.

16. See Rudolf Otto, *The Idea of the Holy,* trans. John W. Harvey (Oxford: Oxford University Press, 1923).

17. See David Peterson, *Possessed by God: A New Testament Theology of Sanctification and Holiness* (Leicester: IVP/Apollos, 1995).

18. Gordon J. Thomas, "A Holy God Among a Holy People in a Holy Place: The Enduring Eschatological Hope," in Kent E. Brower and Mark W. Elliott, eds., *The Reader Must Understand: Eschatology in Bible and Theology* (Leicester: IVP/Apollos, 1997), 53-69. (Published in North America as *Eschatology in Bible and Theology: Evangelical Essays at the Dawn of a New Millennium* [Downers Grove, Ill.: InterVarsity Press, 1997].) All references are to the North American edition.

19. Word study is the starting point for those older saints who complain that their minister hasn't preached "holiness" for years because they have not heard the words "entire sanctification" in his or her sermons. Even the very valuable work by William M. Greathouse, *Wholeness in Christ: Toward a Biblical Theology of Holiness* (Kansas City: Beacon Hill Press of Kansas City, 1998), 11-16, starts at this point but attempts to consider the words in their context.

20. The crucial text here is James Barr, *The Semantics of Biblical Language* (Oxford: Oxford University Press, 1961).

21. See the articles by K. E. Brower on "Holiness" and "Sanctification" in the *New Bible Dictionary,* rev. ed. (Leicester: IVP, 1996), 477-78, 1057-59.

22. K. E. Brower, "'Let the Reader Understand': Temple and Eschatology in Mark," in *Eschatology,* eds. Brower, Elliott, 120 n. 3.

23. See Michael Lodahl, *The Story of God* (Kansas City: Beacon Hill Press of Kansas City, 1997).

24. See Pinnock, *Flame of Love,* 225-26, who suggests, "Revelation is conveyed in the story of the mighty acts of God. . . . It is the dynamic self-disclosure of God, who makes his goodness known in the history of salvation, in a process of disclosure culminating in Jesus Christ." See also G. E. Wright, *The Acts of God: Biblical Theology as Recital,* Studies in Biblical Theology (SBT) 8 (London: SCM, 1952), for an example of the attention given to biblical theology by an earlier generation of scholars. After a moribund period of two or more decades, a renewed interest in biblical theology has emerged in the latter part of the 20th century.

25. G. B. Caird and L. D. Hurst, *New Testament Theology* (Oxford: Clarendon, 1995), 348.

26. Standard treatments of the "doctrine of God" usually begin with a monistic picture of God and only comes to a Trinitarian view at the end rather than the beginning with God as Trinity. See, for example, Alister McGrath, *Understanding the Trinity* (Eastbourne, U.K.: Kingsway, 1986). Perhaps quite properly for this topic in this series, McGrath moves to his discussion of Trinity as the conclusion.

27. For a select bibliography of recent work on the Trinity, see David S. Cunningham, *These Three Are One: The Practice of Trinitarian Theology* (Oxford: Blackwell, 1998), 339-42. To this list should be added Colin E. Gunton, *The Triune Creator* (Edinburgh: Edinburgh University Press, 1998), *Christ and Creation,* 1990 Didsbury Lectures (Carlisle, U.K.: Paternoster, 1993) and *The Promise of Trinitarian Theology,* 2nd ed. (Edinburgh: T & T Clark, 1997).

28. An examination of the biblical basis for each of these teachings has produced a vast literature, including the agenda-setting work of J. D. G. Dunn, *The Baptism of the Spirit: A Re-examination of the New Testament Teaching on the Gift of the Spirit in Relation to Pentecostalism Today* (London: SCM, 1970). See also Roger Stronstad, *The Charismatic Theology of St. Luke* (Peabody, Mass.: Hendrickson, 1984), R. P. Menzies, *Empowered for Witness: The Spirit in Luke-Acts* (Sheffield, U.K.: SAP, 1994), M. M. B. Turner, *Power from On High* (Sheffield, U.K.: SAP, 1996), and *The Holy Spirit and Spiritual Gifts Then and Now* (Carlisle, U.K.: Paternoster, 1996).

29. The expulsion of Jews (leaders?) from Rome under Claudius in A.D. 49 is plausibly explained as an intra-Jewish debate over the messianic claims of Christians. See Seutonius, *Life of Claudius* 25.4.

30. See Richard Bauckham, ed., *The Gospel for All Christians: Rethinking the Gospel Audiences* (Edinburgh: T & T Clark, 1998). Bauckham, 4, writes, "The Matthean, Markan, Lukan and Johannine communities should disappear from the terminology of Gospels scholarship."

31. Richard Bauckham, "For whom were the Gospels written?" in ibid., 46.

32. Two recent studies are particularly helpful and accessible. They are by Hannah Harrington, *Holiness: Rabbinic Judaism and the Graeco-Roman World* (London/New York: Routledge, 2001) and L. W. Hurtado, *At the Origins of Christian Worship*, 1999 Didsbury Lectures (Carlisle, U.K.: Paternoster, 2000). This whole section is indebted to the work of these scholars.

33. Hurtado, *Origins*, 12.

34. Ibid., 8.

35. Harrington, *Holiness*, 10.

36. See ibid., 19-20.

37. Harrington, *Holiness*, 20.

38. Hurtado, *Origins*, 21.

39. Harrington, *Holiness*, 45.

40. In Greece, inheritance of the position was usual although purchase was also an option; good family background the usual qualification. It was a distinct honor to be a priest—salary and housing, exemptions from some obligations, complimentary passes at theater; upper-class social status. Although some cults allowed women to serve as priests, thus greatly enhancing their status, women usually served female deities. High priests usually had many restrictions and sacred taboos, not unlike the Israelite high priest. See ibid., 66-69.

41. Harrington, *Holiness*, 58.

42. Ibid., 142.

43. The only exception of written sacred texts were the Sybilline Oracles (from 6th century B.C.E. prophetess Cumaean Sibyl), but these were mainly predictions. See ibid., 138.

44. Harrington, *Holiness*, 114.

45. Ibid., 161.

46. Ibid., 55.

47. Second Temple Judaism refers to Judaism in ancient Jewish history between Ezra and the destruction of the Temple in Jerusalem in A.D. 70.

48. See, for example, Hartley, *Leviticus*, lvii.

49. See ibid., lvii.

50. See Philip Jenson, *Graded Holiness: A Key to the Priestly Conception of the*

*World* (Journal for the Study of the Old Testament Supplement Series 106) (Sheffield, U.K.: SAP, 1993).

51. See Hartley, *Leviticus,* lxiii.

52. Scot McKnight, *A New Vision for Israel: The Teachings of Jesus in National Context* (Grand Rapids: Eerdmans, 1999), 24.

53. Thomas, "A Holy God," 58.

54. This problem lies at the heart of Paul's debate on "works of the law." It has plagued the Holiness Movement from its inception.

55. See Thomas, "A Holy God," 59.

56. We have some difficulty in thinking this way. In our minds, a group is made up of individuals. Individuals may or may not belong to a group. But the biblical perspective is that individuals exist only in a group.

57. This is one of the major and more controversial points proposed by N. T. Wright, *Jesus and the Victory of God,* vol. 2 of *Christian Origins and the Question of God* (London: SPCK, 1993), passim. Hereinafter referred to as JVG. See the further support offered by Craig A. Evans, "Jesus and the Continuing Exile of Israel," *Jesus and the Restoration of Israel,* ed. Carey C. Newman (Carlisle, U.K./Downers Grove, Ill.: Paternoster/IVP, 1999), 77-100.

58. See especially N. T. Wright, *The New Testament and the People of God,* vol. 1 of *Christian Origins and the Question of God* (London: SPCK, 1992), passim, for the full details of this picture. Hereinafter referred to as NTPG.

59. See especially Ezek. 36:25-27 and Jer. 31:31-34.

60. See Isa. 66:8-23; Mal. 3—4.

61. The Temple in Jesus' time was Herod's major achievement and, perhaps, the source of his claim to be the rightful occupant of the throne of David. See W. Horbury, "Herod's Temple and 'Herod's Days,'" *Templum Amicitiae,* ed. W. Horbury (Journal for the Study of the New Testament Supplement Series 48; Sheffield, U.K.: JSOT, 1991).

62. Wright, JVG, 411.

63. Similar to the use of "Downing Street," "The White House," or "The Kremlin" as a cipher for the prime minister or president.

64. Wright, JVG, 406.

65. See Brower, "Temple and Eschatology" in *Eschatology.*

66. The designation is from J. D. G. Dunn, *The Partings of the Ways* (London/Harrisburg: SCM/Trinity, 1991).

67. But without a temple [exile, post 70] the Torah became the central point. As Wright observes, "For millions of ordinary Jews, Torah became a portable Land, a movable Temple" (NTPG, 228).

68. Marcus J. Borg, *Conflict, Holiness, and Politics in the Teachings of Jesus,* rev. ed. (Harrisburg, Pa.: Trinity, 1998; first edition 1984), 68.

69. Ibid., 71. The importance of both Torah and Temple led, inevitably, to the interpretation and application of Torah into the rules leading to Mishnah. But the Mishnah never had the status of Torah. See Wright, NTPG, 230.

70. The meaning of the phrase "works of the law" is disputed in Pauline studies. Some, such as J. D. G. Dunn, argue that it refers to the making and keeping of these nationalistic identity markers. Others argue that it refers more generally to scrupulous keeping of the Law in general by observant second Temple Jews.

71. Wright, NTPG, 238.

72. Ibid., 279. Wright and a number of other scholars of the so-called Third

Quest have been profoundly influential on my thinking in this whole area. The following summary is heavily dependent upon their analysis.

73. Ibid.

74. The term belongs to E. P. Sanders.

75. See especially Wright, NTPG, 187 ff.

76. See ibid., 190 ff., for some of the evidence.

77. Borg, *Conflict, Holiness, and Politics,* 74.

78. Ibid., 81.

79. Wright, NTPG, 187.

80. Borg, *Conflict, Holiness, and Politics,* 76.

81. This section is heavily dependent upon the excellent work of A. R. G. Deasley, *The Shape of Qumran Theology,* 1985 Didsbury Lectures (Carlisle, U.K.: Paternoster, 2000). Since the discovery of the Dead Sea Scrolls in 1948, growing understanding
of their thought and practice, as well as considerable enhancement of our understanding of the second Temple period, has flowed from the extensive scholarly attention to
these remarkable texts.

82. The term "Qumran" is used here to refer to the community of people whose
beliefs and practices are known from the Dead Sea Scrolls.

83. Deasley, *Shape of Qumran Theology,* 218. Deasley gives full citations of the
texts supporting his views throughout his thorough treatment of the scrolls. Reference
should be made to his annotations.

84. Wright, NTPG, 205.

85. Deasley, *Shape of Qumran Theology,* 239.

86. Borg, *Conflict, Holiness, and Politics,* 72.

87. See 1QS 6.13b-23 and Deasley, *Shape of Qumran Theology,* 217.

88. See 1QS 3.9.

89. 1QS 8.9, 21.

90. Deasley, *Shape of Qumran Theology,* 210.

91. Ibid., 233.

92. Ibid., 234.

93. Ibid., 210-11.

94. Ibid., 226, citing F. F. Bruce.

95. Ibid., 238.

96. Ibid., 225 ff.

97. Ibid., 230-31.

98. Ibid., 232.

99. Ibid., 244.

100. Ibid., 240.

101. Ibid., 244.

102. Ibid., 246.

103. Ibid., 325.

104. Wright, NTPG, 208.

105. Borg, *Conflict, Holiness, and Politics,* 96.

106. The details of this discussion appear in K. E. Brower, "The Holy One and His
Disciples: Holiness and Ecclesiology in Mark" in *Holiness and Ecclesiology: Essays on
the "Holy Church,"* ed. K. E. Brower and A. Johnson (Grand Rapids: Eerdmans, forthcoming). See also Luke 7; 19:7-10, 15.

107. See Borg, *Conflict, Holiness, and Politics,* 74-77, 94-96, for a summary of the issues.

108. Ibid., 95.

109. Ibid., 100.

110. Wright, *JVG,* 274.

111. Borg, *Conflict, Holiness, and Politics,* 112.

112. See K. E. Brower, "Jesus and the Lustful Eye: Matthew 5:28," *Evangelical Quarterly* (EQ) 76 (2004), 291-309.

113. Borg, *Conflict, Holiness, and Politics,* 170.

114. Ibid., 146.

115. Ibid., 149.

116. See L. W. Hurtado, *One God, One Lord,* rev ed. (Edinburgh: T & T Clark, 1998) and *Origins.*

117. See the detailed work by Martin Hengel and Anna Maria Schwemer, *Paul Between Damascus and Antioch,* trans. John Bowden (London: SCM, 1997).

118. Chick Yuill, *We Need Saints,* rev. ed. (London: Salvation Army, 1998), 142-43, author's italics.

119. If she married at age 14, a rather common age for marriage in second Temple Judaism, she could well have been in the Temple as a prophet for 60 years. Luke seems quite unaware of the modern claim that the Spirit of prophecy was silent in the intertestamental period

120. Turner, *Power from On High,* 21.

121. Joel B. Green, *The Theology of the Gospel of Luke,* in New Testament Theology series (Cambridge, U.K.: Cambridge University Press, 1995), 39.

122. G. I. Davies, "The Presence of God in the Second Temple and Rabbinic Doctrine," *Templum Amicitiae,* 33, reminds us, "belief in the divine presence in the second-temple was much more widespread than is commonly allowed."

123. Luke seems to be at pains to demonstrate in Acts that the church was put out of the synagogue and not vice versa.

124. For full details of the comparison and contrast between the births of John and Jesus, see R. E. Brown, *The Birth of the Messiah* (New York: Doubleday, 1977).

125. Interestingly enough, according to Luke, the spontaneous joy experienced by the unborn John is frequently experienced by those who are "filled with the Spirit." The association of joy with the presence of the Spirit could help explain why no mention is made of the Spirit in the story of the Ethiopian eunuch in Acts 8:26-40 (but see Luke 24:52, before the outpouring of the Spirit).

126. Attempts to find parallels in other ancient literature have proved to be less than successful. See the literature cited in C. K. Barrett, *The Holy Spirit and the Gospel Tradition* (London: SPCK, 1947, 1966), and J. Nolland, *Luke 1—9:20,* vol. 35A of *Word Biblical Commentary* (WBC) (Dallas: Word, 1989), 43-45.

127. By their very nature, echoes are hard to substantiate, but their identification is crucial for understanding. See Green, *Theology of the Gospel of Luke,* 25.

128. See chap. 3 for further consideration of this notion.

129. Barrett, *Holy Spirit,* 18-23.

130. See R. J. Bauckham, *Jude and the Relatives of Jesus in the Early Church* (Edinburgh: T & T Clark, 1990), 370.

131. Ibid.

132. This does not mean, of course, that Jesus was ever a sinner nor that He was

inherently depraved. Serious work is needed on the doctrine of original sin so that its vital truth about the human condition is not lost in maintaining a biblically unwarranted notion of depravity nor a neutral view of humanity that postulates an equally unbiblical optimism about the human condition. The confusion of fallen flesh with Jesus as a sinner is one of the reasons for the unbiblical and unnecessary Roman Catholic doctrine of the immaculate conception.

133. Nolland, *Luke 1—9:20*, 173.

134. Indeed, the all-too-frequent readiness to account for all of Jesus' experience in terms of His divinity is the bane of popular conservative evangelicalism.

135. See Bauckham, *Jude*, 366, who argues that the genealogy shows that Jesus did not "simply inherit the throne of David: he brings the Davidic monarchy to its eschatological climactic fulfilment."

136. See 4Q246.

137. Joel B. Green, *The Gospel of Luke*, in *New International Commentary on the New Testament* (Grand Rapids/Carlisle, U.K.: Eerdmans/Paternoster, 1997), 90.

138. Turner, *Power from On High*, 24.

139. See Green, *Theology of the Gospel of Luke*, 42.

140. Green, *Gospel of Luke*, 91.

141. Refers to the belief that Jesus' divine Sonship is who He is in essence rather than by adoption.

142. The precise meaning of this statement on the lips of the Baptist is open to debate. See J. D. G. Dunn, "Spirit-and-fire Baptism," *Novum Testamentum* (NovT) 14 (1972), 33-53.

143. See Nolland, *Luke 1—9:20*, 153.

144. Ibid., 160.

145. See I. H. Marshall, "Son of God or Servant of Yahweh? A Reconsideration of Mark 1:11," *New Testament Studies* (NTS) 15 (1968-9), 326-36. See also Green, *Gospel of Luke*, 187.

146. See H. G. M. Williamson, *Variations on a Theme: King, Messiah and Servant in the Book of Isaiah*, the 1997 Didsbury Lectures (Carlisle, U.K.: Paternoster, 1998).

147. Green, *Gospel of Luke*, 187.

148. Gunton, *Christ and Creation*, 81. Gunton goes on to say, "In terms of the imagery of sacrifice, he effects the process of renewal by offering to the Father through the Spirit a cleaned and representative sample of the fallen flesh he bore through being born in a network of corruption."

149. So much so that a previous generation of Lucan scholars developed the "Proto-Luke Hypothesis." To my knowledge, this theory has gone completely out of vogue.

150. Green, *Gospel of Luke*, 191.

151. Graham M. P. McFarlane, *Christ and the Spirit: The Doctrine of the Incarnation According to Edward Irving* (Carlisle, U.K.: Paternoster, 1996), 175.

152. See Walter Wink's important trilogy: *Naming the Powers. The Language of Power in the New Testament; Unmasking the Powers: Forces That Determine Human Existence;* and *Engaging the Powers: Discernment and Resistance in a World of Domination* (Philadelphia: Fortress, 1984, 1986, 1992). See also his recent *When the Powers Fall: Reconciliation Among the Nations* (Minneapolis: Fortress/Augsburg, 1998). Evil is bigger than the sum of its parts, a fact that the past century brought home in horrific ways. The reality it connotes is of an organized system in opposition to God's good purposes that feeds in a parasitic fashion on the evil choices of humans. Hitler,

Stalin, and apartheid only represent scores of manifestations of what could be described as a malevolent incubus.

153. Green, *Gospel of Luke,* 210.

154. See, for example, ibid., 211.

155. Green, *Gospel of Luke,* 212.

156. See now D. D. Swanson, "Re-Minting Christian Holiness." Part 8: "Holiness in Leviticus," *The Flame* 66.1 (2000), 17-19, and a host of other scholars who have drawn attention to this motif in Luke 4:16-20.

157. This section summarizes points already made in K. Brower, "Re-Minting Christian Holiness." Part 13: "The Parables of Jesus," *The Flame* 66.4 (2000), 7-8.

158. Stephen C. Barton, "Parables on God's Love and Forgiveness," *The Challenge of Jesus' Parables,* ed. R. N. Longenecker (Grand Rapids/Cambridge, U.K.: Eerdmans, 2000), 203.

159. Despite the difficulties the masculine personal pronoun in reference to God causes for those who find the language inextricably tied to a patriarchal view of God, with reluctance I continue to use it because I have not found a satisfactory alternative. Nonetheless, I wholly reject the projection of human notions of gender and sexuality upon God and reject the implications for hierarchy and patriarchy that have all too often been drawn by some Christians. See the very brief discussion in Clark H. Pinnock and Robert C. Brow, *Unbounded Love* (Carlisle, U.K.: Paternoster, 1994), 50-51.

160. See J. A. T. Robinson, *The Priority of John* (London: SCM, 1985).

161. It is interesting to note that the liturgy for the Reception of Church Members in the Church of the Nazarene *Manual* states, "We believe in God the Father, Son, and Holy Spirit. We especially emphasize the deity of Jesus Christ and the personality of the Holy Spirit." Against a background that might well have questioned the deity of Jesus Christ, this statement may have been valuable but as a statement of faith it, too, is borderline docetic, with no statement at all of His full humanity.

162. I have personally come to the view that the Trinity needs to be the starting point of Christian theology as well as its conclusion.

163. Except in my home church when a child, where my father was the Sunday School superintendent. In the opening session of our Sunday School, children recited the Apostles' Creed and the Lord's Prayer together every Sunday, a practice long since abandoned.

164. Cunningham, *These Three Are One,* 23.

165. The following summary is developed from Cunningham's helpful survey, *These Three Are One,* 20-30. Cunningham identifies several seminal thinkers, including Karl Barth, Hans Urs von Balthasar, Jürgen Moltmann, Alan Torrance, and Colin E. Gunton among others. In addition to Cunningham, the writing of Gunton is the most accessible.

166. Gunton, *Christ and Creation,* 74.

167. Please supply your own culturally appropriate term.

168. See the apt title of Michael Lodahl's introduction to Wesleyan theology, *The Story of God.*

169. See Cunningham, *These Three Are One,* 84: "There can be no purely natural knowledge of God, for there is no pure nature; the world is not a 'naturally-occurring phenomenon.' It is created, redeemed and sustained by God—in short, it is produced by God. So any knowledge of God that we can glean from the world must also be produced by God."

170. Ibid., 79.

171. Pinnock's *Flame of Love* is subtitled "A Theology of the Holy Spirit," but Spirit is treated in a thoroughly Trinitarian context and with enormous practical implications.

172. See the extended interaction in Moltmann's works, for example, and the renewed interest among Evangelical theologians such as Miroslav Volf. Recent numbers of the *Wesleyan Theological Journal* carry on this conversation while the March 2000 meeting of the Wesleyan Theological Society was devoted to the topic "The Holy Trinity."

173. Cunningham, *These Three Are One*, 27.

174. Cunningham cites Nazianzus' *Theological Orations* 6.11; 6.22; 31.9, τα Τρια.

175. This may well be the underlying difficulty with such diverse derivatives of Christian Trinitarian orthodoxy as Unitarianism, Jehovah's Witnesses, and even English Deism (although the latter is technically Trinitarian). Monotheism construed as singularity is also a major sticking point between Christians and the other two great monotheistic faiths, Islam and Judaism.

176. Cunningham, *These Three Are One*, 181.

177. The work of John D. Zizioulas, *Being as Communion: Studies in Personhood and the Church* (Crestwood, N.Y.: St. Vladimir's Seminary Press, 1993) has been important to theologians. The discussion in this book, however, is dependent upon the work of Gunton.

178. Pinnock, *Flame of Love*, 22. He states that the Christian understanding of God is pure relationality.

179. Kallistos Ware, *The Orthodox Way* (London: Mowbray, 1979), 33.

180. Pinnock, *Flame of Love*, 31

181. Ibid., 29. His use of the term "mutuality" is not my source, but the term is one that I have also found descriptive of the Trinitarian relationship.

182. Cunningham, *These Three Are One*, 57.

183. Genesis, of course, must be read appropriately within its own context and with its own integrity, speaking to its intended audience. But it also needs to be remembered that it functions in an intertextual relationship with the remainder of the Old Testament as well as with the New Testament. Texts used in isolation lead to distortions; texts that are not read contextually all too often disappear into banality through lack of imagination.

184. The NRSV translates *ruach* here as "wind." See Gordon J. Wenham, *Genesis 1—15*, vol. 1 of WBC (Waco, Tex.: Word, 1987), 17, who argues persuasively for "'Wind of God' as a concrete and vivid image of the Spirit of God."

185. Cunningham, *These Three Are One*, 90. See his very helpful assessment of Augustine's thoughts as well as the objections of Barth. These objections are sophisticated but at root they relate to Barth's abhorrence of anything that might point to a "natural theology." But see James Barr, *Biblical Faith and Natural Theology: The 1991 Gifford Lectures* (Oxford: Oxford University Press, 1995).

186. Wenham, *Genesis 1—15*, 14, "It is simply the ordinary word of God. plural in form but singular in meaning."

187. See, for example, Wenham, ibid., 27-28, who notes that the insights of *sensus plenior* were certainly beyond the editor of Genesis. Perhaps, but not all scholars are so cautious.

188. Cunningham, *These Three Are One*, 141.

189. Gunton, *Christ and Creation*, 101.

190. See Cunningham, *These Three Are One*, 142, who notes that "the traditional translation of this word [adam] as 'man' obscures the change that takes place when the creature falls asleep. The English makes it appear that a man falls asleep, and that the same man wakes up (and finds woman beside him). The Hebrew suggests that one kind of being falls asleep, and two wholly different beings wake up." While one should not press this point too far, Cunningham's argument does show that the first and second narratives are complementary.

191. Gunton, *Christ and Creation*, 101-2.

192. Again, although the passage does not have formal Trinitarian language, "in a mysterious manner Spirit may be said to unite the Father and Son in love and to proceed as the love between them" (Pinnock, *Flame of Love*, 38).

193. Pinnock, *Flame of Love*, 39.

194. The specific text is this: "As you, Father, are in me and I am in you, may they also be in us." Unfortunately, most western commentators avoid giving detailed comment on John 17:22-23.

195. Pinnock, *Flame of Love*, 31.

196. Cunningham, *These Three Are One*, 182.

197. Pinnock uses the term "ecstasy" to describe the life in the Spirit.

198. Pinnock, *Flame of Love*, 154.

199. There is also a play on words between "clean" and "prune" that is obscured by our English translations. The disciples are clean, but they will continue to be pruned. See Colin G. Kruse, *John*, in *Tyndale New Testament Commentary* (hereinafter abbreviated TNTC) (Leicester, U.K./Grand Rapids: IVP/Eerdmans, 2003/2004), 316.

200. The use of this phrase in the fourth Gospel is painful in our modern context because of the abusive use of the term by some Christians against Jews. In the fourth Gospel, the Jewish Jesus is confronted by hostility from His fellow Jews and this term is almost always a cipher for those who oppose Him.

201. John 3:16 gives support for the view that the mission is Trinitarian in that it is God who sends the only begotten Son rather than the Father.

202. I am not drawing a great distinction between the words "holiness" and "sanctification." These cognate words can only be separated by context. See Brower, "Sanctification" and "Holiness."

203. Cunningham, *These Three Are One*, 78, states, "the divine missions link the internal divine processions (which constitute God's Triunity) to our experience of God in history."

204. When the dominant model of Atonement is forensic, a static view of imputed righteousness often is a corollary.

205. This section is more fully developed in Brower, "Holiness and Ecclesiology in Mark," forthcoming.

206. This point is picked up in chapter 5.

207. See chapter 1.

208. See the older works by W. Marxsen, *Mark the Evangelist: Studies on the Redaction History of the Gospel*, trans. Roy A. Harrisville, et al. (Nashville/New York: Abingdon, 1969); Ulrich Mauser, *Christ in the Wilderness: The Wilderness Theme in the Second Gospel and Its Basis in the Biblical Tradition*, SBT 39 (London: SCM, 1963). Two important recent studies are by Joel Marcus, *The Way of the Lord: Christological*

*Exegesis of the Old Testament in the Gospel of Mark* (Edinburgh: T & T Clark, 1993); Rikki E. Watts, *Isaiah's New Exodus and Mark* (Tübingen: J. C. B. Mohr [Paul Siebeck], 1997).

209. Ben F. Meyer, *The Aims of Jesus* (London: SCM, 1979), 119.

210. See K. E. Brower, "Elijah in the Markan Passion Narrative," *Journal for the Study of the New Testament* (JSNT) 18 (1983), 85-101. See also Steven M. Bryan, *Jesus and Israel's Traditions of Judgement and Restoration,* Society of New Testament Studies, Monograph Series (SNTSMS) 117 (Cambridge, U.K.: Cambridge University Press, 2002).

211. The issue here, of course, is identity, not ontology. See R. J. Bauckham, *God Crucified,* the 1996 Didsbury Lectures (Carlisle, U.K.: Paternoster, 1998).

212. The picture in Luke is subtly different. See chapter 2 above.

213. See Marshall, "Mark 1:11."

214. See Brower, "Eschatology and Temple," for a discussion of Jesus as the new locale of God's presence among His people.

215. See Meyer, *Aims of Jesus,* 118. An interesting intertextual possibility may be suggested between Isa. 43:19-20, "I am about to do a new thing; now it springs forth, do you not perceive it? I will make a way in the wilderness and rivers in the desert. The wild animals will honor me," with Mark 1:13, "He was in the wilderness forty days, tempted by Satan; and he was with the wild beasts; and the angels waited on him."

216. This might suggest that second Temple Judaism was "dualistic." See, however, discussions of Jewish apocalyptic thought, which suggest that this is only a modified cosmic dualism in which the present age is temporarily held in thralldom to Satan and his powers.

217. The confession by the demons of Jesus' status is one key ingredient in the development of W. Wrede's "messianic secret" hypothesis. See J. D. G. Dunn, "The Messianic Secret in Mark," *The Messianic Secret, Issues in Religion and Theology* (IRT) 1, ed. C. M. Tuckett (London/Philadelphia: SCM/Fortress, 1983), 116-31.

218. Contra Edwin K. Broadhead, *Naming Jesus: Titular Christology in the Gospel of Mark* (Journal for the Study of the New Testament Supplement Series [JSNTSS] 175; Sheffield, U.K.: SAP, 1999), 100, who calls it "an isolated and largely inconsequential description." The only other Gospel usage is John 6:68-69 where the confession is on the lips of Simon Peter. Explicit usage in the Old Testament is also rare.

219. L. W. Hurtado, *Lord Jesus Christ: Devotion to Jesus in Earliest Christianity* (Grand Rapids/Cambridge, U.K.: Eerdmans, 2003), 287, writes, "One of the several Markan uses of irony is that the demons, those powers that Jesus comes to destroy, recognize Jesus' transcendent status."

220. "Son of the Blessed One" is a circumlocution for "Son of God."

221. Debates about whether the phrase should be translated as "a son of god" or "the Son of God" are interesting but ultimately fruitless. The very ambiguity of the Greek phrase tells against any view that the centurion had much more in mind than the experience of watching "a good death." See now R. T. France, *The Gospel of Mark,* in *New International Greek Testament Commentary* (NIGTC) (Grand Rapids/Carlisle, U.K.: Eerdmans/Paternoster, 2002), 659-60.

222. Equally, Mark's use of this term should not be read against the background of the later Christian reflection on the phrase. Broadhead, 162, quite correctly argues that the phrase in this instance "stands at a crucial juncture between the generalised images of the historical background and the confessional certainty of early Christianity."

223. But in 9:3-10, the voice is from a cloud, likely an allusion to the cloud as the presence of God (see especially Exodus).

224. Debate about whether this opening phrase is an introduction to the prologue, the limits of which itself are disputed, or the whole gospel continue. On literary grounds alone, the latter is the more likely.

225. Ἀρχὴ τοῦ εὐαγγελίου Ἰησοῦ Χριστοῦ (υἱοῦ θεοῦ). Although the words υἱοῦ θεοῦ may be disputed on textual grounds alone, on literary grounds they should be included. See, however, Peter M. Head, "A Text-Critical Study of Mark 1:1 'The Beginning of the Gospel of Jesus Christ,'" NTS 37 (1991), 621-29, who argues against reading "Son of God" as the original text.

226. Some prefer to use "followership" rather than "discipleship," arguing that the former term better captures the dynamic sense of relationship to Jesus in which the disciple never becomes the master. But "discipleship" as used in this chapter includes both the call and the following. Discipleship is both a matter of being a disciple and following the master.

227. The exception is R. H. Gundry, *A Commentary on His Apology for the Cross* (Grand Rapids: Eerdmans, 1993).

228. This is a favorite word of Mark's.

229. A great deal of discussion has been devoted to the question on whether the proper translation is "is near" or "has arrived," with an earlier generation of scholars concentrating on the meaning of ἤγγικεν. But the context of the gospel and restoration eschatology in the second Temple period tell decisively in favor of "has arrived."

230. We can reasonably assume that they were observant, pious Jews of the second Temple period, perhaps even thinking of themselves as part of God's righteous remnant. They may have been part of John's entourage, people who had repented and been baptized by John (see John 1:35-42). If so, they knew, or knew about, Jesus. Perhaps they were already part of a restoration movement such as John's. Perhaps they had even listened to Jesus' teaching. But if any of this is so, Mark doesn't tell us. His focus lies elsewhere.

231. Few specific examples of Old Testament models for understanding the relationship between Jesus and His disciples are available. But the key (Gen. 12:1-3) text shows Abraham following God not knowing where he is going, a pattern remembered in Heb. 11:8. The journey motif is dominant in the Old Testament for the people of God.

232. See Luke 22:30. See also 1 Cor. 6:2 where Paul reminds the saints that they are to judge the world, not to mention angels. Their designation as "the Twelve" may also signal that they have more significance as a group than as individuals who are formed into a group. We rarely hear of them as individuals (but see 14:29-30; 16:7).

233. Mark, in my estimation, is a master storyteller. He uses two-level narration throughout this Gospel. On the one hand, we have the level of the story at which the persons in the story all function. But the second level is the story within the story, the level of what was going on in what happened. Jesus functions at both levels; so does the author and so do we as readers. To accomplish this literary task, Mark uses three techniques: inclusio, intercalation, and prefiguring. Inclusio occurs when Mark brackets one text between two others. Together these texts serve to interpret one another. Intercalation occurs when a continuous narrative is interrupted by another text in a "meanwhile, back at the ranch" fashion. Progression or prefiguring occurs throughout the narrative. This story is written in inclusio form.

234. See E. P. Sanders, *Jesus and Judaism* (London: SCM, 1985).

235. This riposte, of course, contains a veiled warning to the leaders that their opposition to Him will ultimately bring down the nation. See Wright, JVG. See also Brower, "Eschatology and Temple."

236. See D. D. Swanson, "Offerings for Sin in Leviticus and John Wesley's Definition," *European Explorations in Christian Holiness* 1 (1999), 9-22.

237. See Willard Swartley, *Mark: The Way for All Nations* (Scottdale, Pa.: Herald, 1981), for a helpful discussion on the path of discipleship in Mark and for this point in particular.

238. The phrase "on the way" or something similar occurs more than a dozen times in this section.

239. The Matthean Jesus describes the answer given by Peter on behalf of them all as a miracle of revelation from God (Matt. 16:16).

240. See K. E. Brower, "Mark 9:1—Seeing the Kingdom in Power," JSNT 6 (1980), 17-41.

241. See Brower, "Elijah," 85-101, for a discussion of the significance of Elijah's presence here.

242. "Proper technique" may lie behind a very early reading of the story reflected in an ancient strand of the textual tradition, which adds "and fasting."

243. Here an ancient strand of the textual tradition adds an additional "who does not follow us," adding strength to the view here propounded.

244. Chapter 10 contains some of the most challenging and interesting ethical teaching on two particularly relevant issues for today—the issues of divorce and wealth. Neither of these points can be touched upon in the context of this chapter.

245. See Matt. 19:28-29 and Luke 18:28-30.

246. Please supply your own equivalents.

247. See Brower, "Eschatology and Temple," for a discussion of the place of the Temple in Mark's theology. The following two sections are edited versions of part of this article.

248. The first question, asked by a Sadducee concerning the Resurrection, is in 12:18-27.

249. The whole section is pervaded by a growing sense of conflict with the Temple establishment. Thus, we have chief priests, scribes, elders, Pharisees, Herodians, and Sadducees all in opposition to Jesus. See Wright, NTPG, 210-12.

250. To say, in the Temple and following Jesus' prophetic representative action in the Temple, that these commandments given by Jesus are more than all whole burnt offerings and sacrifices, brings the whole sequence to its point.

251. Wright, JVG, 566.

252. Earlier studies sought to establish the unity of the so-called Little Apocalypse. See, for example, G. R. Beasley-Murray, *Jesus and the Future: An Examination of the Criticism of the Eschatological Discourse, Mark 13 with Special Reference to the Little Apocalypse Theory* (London: Macmillan, 1954), and David Wenham, *The Rediscovery of Jesus' Eschatological Discourse, Gospel Perspectives* 4 (Sheffield: JSOT, 1984).

253. T. J. Geddert, *Watchwords: Mark 13 in Markan Eschatology*, JSNTSS 26 (Sheffield: JSOT, 1989), 146, argues that "Mark 13 is an anti-temple speech; it is not a speech introduced by a few unimportant references to the temple and then proceeding with total disregard for the temple and its fate."

254. An inclusio of 13:5, "then Jesus began to say to them," with 13:37, 'and what I say to you I say to all,' shows that Mark has his implied readers in view. The call to cross-bearing in 8:34-38 likewise extends beyond the historical first disciples, but here, the teaching is even more clearly directed to the readers.

255. R. H. Lightfoot, *The Gospel Message of St. Mark* (Oxford: Oxford University Press, 1950), 48-59.

256. Paula Fredriksen, *From Jesus to Christ: The Origins of the New Testament Images of Jesus* (New Haven, Conn.: Yale, 1988), 50.

257. P. G. Bolt, "Mark 13: An Apocalyptic Precursor to the Passion Narrative," *Reformed Theological Review* 54 (1995), for example, argues that Mark 13 finds fulfill-ment in the passion and exaltation of Jesus. Bolt is probably right to see "this genera-tion" (13:30; see also 9:1) as pointing to events in the narrative itself. There is a future element in chapter 13 that extends beyond the immediately following passion narra-tive but that does not extend indefinitely into the future. Hence, those who hold that the primary referent in this chapter is to the destruction of the Temple give greater co-herence to the narrative as a whole.

258. Geddert, *Watchwords,* 109.

259. Ibid., 255.

260. Failure and restoration is an important theme in the Old Testament, not just by those who turn away from God's purposes, but also by the people of God's own heart—Abraham and David are two of the most prominent. See especially Ps. 78 where the picture of God's ongoing grace is seen in the context of Israel's failure.

261. In Mark's scheme of things, Judas does not receive the attention he is given in the later Gospels (see 14:10-11, 21). The crucial difference in Judas' betrayal is that he goes to those whose opposition to Jesus is implacable. Judas, therefore, goes "out-side" and fits in with those who accuse Jesus of acting in the power of Beelzebul (3:20-30) and who ultimately reject Jesus and His path. Peter, by contrast, does not re-ject Jesus.

262. The ending of Mark has been a debate among scholars for some time. Literar-ily, it is possible to argue two ways. First, some might say that the narrative demands an appearance of the risen Lord as the fitting denouement. But the narrative can also be seen to end in a deliberately open-ended fashion that implies that the story continues.

263. From Mark, it would be very difficult to establish any interest in describing the ordo salutis; the nature of discipleship does not lend itself to this kind of structure.

264. Georg Strecker, *The Sermon on the Mount: An Exegetical Commentary,* trans. O. C. Dean Jr. (Nashville: Abingdon, 1988), 11.

265. The history of the interpretation of the Sermon on the Mount before 1975 is set out in W. S. Kissinger, *The Sermon on the Mount: A History of Interpretation and Bibliography* (Metuchen, N.J.: Scarecrow, 1975). For details of more recent work, see the extensive discussion in H. D. Betz, *The Sermon on the Mount: A Commentary on the Sermon on the Mount, including the Sermon on the Plain (Matthew 5:3—7:27 and Luke 6:20-49), Hermeneia* (Minneapolis: Fortress, 1995), 1-89. See also the commen-taries by Craig S. Keener, *A Commentary on the Gospel of Matthew* (Grand Rapids/ Cambridge, U.K.: Eerdmans, 1990); Donald A. Hagner, *Matthew 1—13,* WBC 33A (Dallas: Word, 1993); and W. D. Davies and D. C. Allison, *A Critical and Exegetical Commentary on the Gospel According to Saint Matthew: 1—7,* ICC (Edinburgh: T & T Clark, 1988).

266. Dale C. Allison, *The New Moses: A Matthean Typology* (Edinburgh: T & T

Clark, 1993), 274, calls Matthew's use of the Old Testament the "antithesis of Marcionitism."

267. See Robert H. Gundry, *The Use of the Old Testament in St. Matthew's Gospel, Supplements to Novum Testamentum* (NovTSup) 18 (Leiden, Neth.: E. J. Brill, 1967), for a full analysis of the formula citations from, and allusions to, the Old Testament in Matthew. See also Krister Stendahl, *The School of St. Matthew and Its Use of the Old Testament,* rev. ed. (Philadelphia: Fortress, 1968).

268. The classic study is that of B. W. Bacon, *Studies in Matthew* (New York: Holt, 1930).

269. Davies and Allison, *Matthew: 1 — 7,* 58-72.

270. Dale C. Allison, "The Structure of the Sermon on the Mount," *Journal of Biblical Literature* (JBL) 106 (1987), 423-45.

271. See W. D. Davies, *The Setting of the Sermon on the Mount* (Cambridge, U.K.: Cambridge University Press, 1964) and now Betz, *Sermon.*

272. See Robert A. Guelich, *The Sermon on the Mount* (Waco, Tex.: Word, 1982), for a judicious use of structure in clarifying meaning. Guelich's analysis has been especially influential in this chapter.

273. See Brown, *Birth,* for a detailed consideration of these two sections.

274. The historical questions need not detain us; our purpose is more theological, that is, "What is Matthew trying to tell his readers about this Jesus and His significance?"

275. See R. T. France, *The Gospel According to Matthew,* TNTC (Leicester, U.K.: InterVarsity Press, 1985), and R. T. France, *Matthew: Evangelist and Teacher* (Carlisle, U.K.: Paternoster, 1989).

276. The inclusion of four women and some rather dubious relationships is important. Davies and Allison note "irregular and potentially scandalous unions, even unions with Gentiles, were blessed by God in establishing and continuing the Davidic line. Thus if the birth of Jesus also involved extraordinary circumstances and brought reproach, that was nothing new. Rather was it foreshadowed in the unions of Joseph and Tamar, Salmon and Rahab, Boaz and Ruth, David and Bathsheba" (187-88). The key point is probably, however, that these are all either Gentile women by birth or by marriage (see Ulrich Luz, *The Theology of the Gospel of Matthew,* New Testament Theology series (NTT), trans. J. Bradford Robinson (Cambridge, U.K.: Cambridge University Press, 1995), 26. Other motifs could include the variety of ways in which God's good purposes can be accomplished, even, it must be noted, despite having to work through the progeny of a relationship that started as a rape (David of Bathsheba).

277. Davies and Allison, *Matthew: 1 — 7,* 165, think the best explanation for the three sets of 14 generations is *gematria* based upon "David." See F. D. Bruner, *The Christbook Matthew 1 — 12,* vol. 1 of *Matthew: A Commentary* (Grand Rapids/Carlisle, U.K.: Eerdmans/Paternoster, 2004, rev. and expanded ed.), 7-22. Bruner, 22, warns against "excessive attention to complex numbers or to strange details—that is, tricky theology [because it] . . . has contributed to theological aberrations" among which he identifies much "prophetic teaching" and some forms of dispensationalism.

278. Hagner, *Matthew 1 — 13,* 9. Davies and Allison, *Matthew: 1 — 7,* who think that it might go back as far as the first century B.C. but was "by the time of Jesus, the dominant, although not exclusive, Jewish expectation," are more cautious (156).

279. See Rom. 1:3-4 for this designation in what is probably a pre-Pauline Christian formulation.

280. In fact, the actions of Joseph in chapter 1 show that he accepts Jesus as his own son.

281. The interpretation of these words is uncertain. See Luz, *Theology*, 24.

282. See Davies and Allison, *Matthew: 1—7*, 159.

283. David D. Kupp, *Matthew's Emmanuel: Divine Presence and God's People in the First Gospel*, SNTSMS 90 (Cambridge, U.K.: Cambridge University Press, 1996), 58.

284. See Williamson, *Variations*, for a discussion of the Isaianic hope that informed the thinking of second Temple Judaism.

285. See details on marriage customs in the second Temple period in Léonie J. Archer, *Her Price Is Beyond Rubies: The Jewish Woman in Graeco-Roman Palestine*, JSOTS60 (Sheffield, U.K.: JSSOT, 1990). Marriage had three parts: bride price; formal document; sexual intercourse. At the time of Mary, evidence suggests that there were two stages. First, betrothal (formal consent before witnesses). At this stage the girl remained in her father's house. Sexual intercourse was not permitted at this stage; in any case, the betrothed was often prepubescent. Virginity was highly valued. Adultery could, however, occur. Hence, Joseph's decision quietly to divorce Mary when she was found to be pregnant. Second, marriage (girl taken in to the groom's family home). Girls were normally married by age 12.5, immediately after puberty.

286. See Kupp, *Matthew's Emmanuel*, 58.

287. Ibid., 54.

288. See ibid., 58, "in fulfilment of the prophet's words a people will in the future call Jesus 'Emmanuel,' recognizing in his salvation that 'God is with us.'"

289. The usual date for the Gospel of Matthew is set after the Fall of Jerusalem, that is, after A.D. 70.

290. Matthew adds a similar phrase to the "words of institution" in 26:28 (cf. Mark 14:24) and adds the phrase "in spirit" to the first beatitude (5:3) to similar effect. This emphasis is far clearer in Matthew than in Luke, where the canticles in the birth narratives might possibly be read in terms of violent revolution.

291. Bruner, *Matthew*, 71, thinks that the lesson of Herod is that "Herod lives on in us, *the people of God*" (author's italics). Here his indebtedness to the Lutheran two-kingdom theology is apparent.

292. The fact that the best estimates suggest that about 20 males under two would be slaughtered does not lessen the horror. Although no external confirmation of this massacre is extant, Herod's behavior here is entirely in keeping with what we know of him from other sources.

293. See Davies and Allison, *Matthew: 1—7*, 268, for a plausible explanation of this process.

294. Hagner, *Matthew 1—13*, 31.

295. Allison, *New Moses*, 140. See pp. 140-65 for his examination of all possible links.

296. Davies and Allison, *Matthew: 1—7*, 282.

297. Hagner, *Matthew 1—13*, 42.

298. Contra Hagner, *Matthew 1—13*, 54, who sees the real point being the threads of continuity and discontinuity between John and Jesus.

299. See J. A. Ziesler, *The Meaning of Righteousness in Paul: A Linguistic and Theological Enquiry*, SNTSMS 20 (Cambridge, U.K.: Cambridge University Press, 1972), whose important study discusses the Old Testament background to the term "righteousness" and established its relational meaning.

300. See Hagner, *Matthew 1—13,* 56.

301. Ibid., 57. Contra Davies and Allison, who think that Jesus is obediently ful-filling messianic prophecies. While this view is correct in general, it does not seem to apply specifically to this particular act.

302. Allison, *New Moses,* 166, thinks the link between Jesus and Moses is strong here, especially with sufficient attention given to the phrase "forty days and forty nights."

303. See Birger Gerhardsson, *The Testing of God's Son (Matt. 4:1–11 & Parallels),* Coniectanea Biblica, New Testament Series (ConBNT) 2.1 (Lund: Gleerup, 1966).

304. Meyer, *Aims of Jesus,* 130.

305. Ulrich Luz, *Matthew 1—7: A Commentary,* trans. W. C. Linss (Minneapolis/ Edinburgh: Fortress/T & T Clark, 1989/1990), 198.

306. Davies and Allison, *Matthew: 1—7,* 390.

307. Meyer, *Aims of Jesus,* 131.

308. Guelich uses these three plus ethical, *Sermon on the Mount,* 27-33.

309. Ibid., 28.

310. See ibid., 29.

311. See Davies and Allison, *Matthew: 1—7,* 413.

312. J. D. Kingsbury, *Matthew,* 3d ed. (Nappanee, Ind.: Evangel, 1998), 46-47 (author's italics).

313. Luz, *Theology,* 43.

314. Few scholars are able to draw a clear distinction between the two—at most one might suggest that preaching is more narrowly focused upon announcing the Kingdom with a view to conversion while teaching includes announcement and cate-chesis, but the distinction is not always clear. See Keener, *Commentary on the Gospel of Matthew,* 155.

315. They are not proofs of divinity, as some have erroneously thought.

316. See Guelich, *Sermon,* 85-87, for an excellent excursus on righteousness in Matthew.

317. See Hagner, *Matthew 1—13,* 93.

318. Guelich, *Sermon,* 87.

319. See H. Benedict Green, *Matthew, Poet of the Beatitudes,* JSNTSS 203 (Shef-field, U.K.: SAP, 2001), 230-31, who argues that this is not pointing to righteousness as God's righteousness but to obedience.

320. See Bruner, *Matthew,* 168.

321. Davies and Allison, *Matthew: 1—7,* 453.

322. See ibid., 451.

323. The reading that suggests Paul's only emphasis is upon the God who justifies the ungodly and does not transform them is open to serious question. Matthew and Paul may not be so far apart on this point as some might imagine.

324. Bruner, *Matthew,* 170.

325. See Hagner, *Matthew 1—13,* 93.

326. Bruner, *Matthew,* 170.

327. Ibid., 171.

328. So Davies and Allison, *Matthew: 1—7,* 453.

329. See section 2.4 below.

330. Guelich, *Sermon,* 87.

331. The riches of the *Book of Common Prayer* capture this thought in the prayer

that reads "Almighty God, unto whom all hearts are open, all desires known, and from whom no secrets are hid; Cleanse the thoughts of our hearts by the inspiration of thy Holy Spirit that we may perfectly love thee, and worthily magnify thy holy Name, through Christ our Lord. *Amen."*

332. See Benedict Green, *Matthew, Poet of the Beatitudes,* 239.

333. See Bruner, *Matthew,* 175, and Benedict Green, *Matthew, Poet of the Beatitudes,* 240.

334. See Bruner, *Matthew,* 176.

335. Ibid., 175.

336. For a full discussion of this verse, see K. E. Brower, "Blessed are the pure in heart," *Biblical Resources for Holiness Preachers,* vol. 2 (Kansas City: Beacon Hill Press of Kansas City, 1995), 15-26.

337. See chapter 1 above for the debate between Jesus and the Pharisees. See Borg, *Conflict,* for a thorough analysis of the holiness debate. M. A. Powell, *Jesus as a Figure in History: How Modern Historians View the Man from Galilee* (Louisville, Ky.: Westminster/John Knox, 1998), 108, states that Borg's view is that "the movement that Jesus initiated was essentially a counterculture association that deliberately defied the politics of holiness." As argued above, Borg draws an unnecessary contrast between holiness and compassion. Holiness properly expresses itself in love and mission. Indeed, the parallel to Matt. 5:48 in Luke 6:36 uses the word "merciful" in place of "perfect," capturing the community-centered compassion that lies at the heart of Jesus' command.

338. McKnight, *A New Vision for Israel,* 24.

339. See Luz, *Theology,* 47.

340. Keener, *Commentary on the Gospel of Matthew,* 175.

341. Sanders, *Jesus and Judaism,* 261, is only one of many scholars who solve the problem by suggesting that Matt. 5:17-19 comes from the Early Church, rather than the historical Jesus; others attempt to separate tradition from redaction, but there is little overall gain from these strategies. (See Guelich, *Sermon,* 134-53.)

342. Meyer, *Aims of Jesus,* 80.

343. Hagner, *Matthew 1—13,* 108.

344. Keener, *Commentary on the Gospel of Matthew,* 162, my italics.

345. See E. P. Sanders, *Paul and Palestinian Judaism* (London: SCM, 1977).

346. Guelich, *Sermon,* 142.

347. Hagner, *Matthew 1—13,* 108, author's italics. See France, *Matthew,* TNCT, 114 who opts for this after considering other alternatives.

348. Keener, *Commentary on the Gospel of Matthew,* 175.

349. A recent tragic example known to me personally involved self-inflicted blindness based upon 5:29.

350. Most interpreters have a curious mixture of literal legalistic reading of the antitheses (for example, 5:32) combined with a rather less literal reading of other sections (vv. 38-44).

351. Betz, *Sermon,* 184.

352. See ibid., 188-89. Betz wonders if that conflict is also behind the next statement about the "least in the kingdom," as the sobriquet of the apostle Paul who seems to teach people to set aside the minutiae of the Law. But see Hagner, *Matthew 1—13,* 109, who considers this "highly improbable."

353. See France, *Matthew,* 115.

354. Crispin H. T. Fletcher-Louis, "The Destruction of the Temple and the Relativization of the Old Covenant: Mark 13:31 and Matthew 5:18," in Brower and Elliott, *Eschatology in Bible and Theology,* 151.

355. Ibid., 165. See also Brower, "Seeing the Kingdom," for a similar view of Mark 9:1.

356. Most scholars do not take this view seriously, however. Keener, *Commentary on the Gospel of Matthew,* 178, for example, rather too hastily cites Overman's dismissive critique.

357. So Luz, *Matthew,* 269.

358. Allison, *New Moses,* 185.

359. So Strecker, *Sermon on the Mount,* 60.

360. Allison, *New Moses,* 323.

361. Luz, *Theology,* 48.

362. Guelich, *Sermon,* 29.

363. Wright, JVG, 289.

364. See Guelich, *Sermon,* 29.

365. Meyer, *Aims of Jesus,* 143. The pattern is repeated throughout Jesus' teaching (see, for example, Mark 10:1-12, where He sees His more radical demands as a return to the creation order).

366. Guelich, *Sermon,* 29.

367. M. D. Hooker, *Continuity and Discontinuity* (London: Epworth, 1986), 31.

368. W. D. Davies, *The Setting of the Sermon on the Mount* (Cambridge, U.K.: Cambridge University Press, 1963), 211, suggests that two orders of Christian is, at first sight, the natural way in which to take verse 21, but notes that this interpretation is unlikely. The whole discussion in Davies, 211-15, is helpful.

369. See chapter 1 above.

370. France, *Matthew,* 286.

371. Davies, *Setting of the Sermon on the Mount,* 211-12.

372. Gerhard Barth, "Matthew's Understanding of the Law"; Günther Bornkamm, Gerhard Barth, and Heinz Joachim Held, *Tradition and Interpretation in Matthew,* trans. Percy Scott (London: SCM, 1963), 95-99.

373. Barth, 99.

374. France, 286, his emphasis.

375. Keener, 531.

376. Luz, *Matthew 1-7,* 269.

# BIBLIOGRAPHY

## Articles Cited

"Re-Minting Christian Holiness" articles on http://holiness.nazarene.ac.uk

Allison, Dale C. "The Structure of the Sermon on the Mount," *Journal of Biblical Literature* (JBL) 106 (1987), 423-45.

Barth, Gerhard. "Matthew's Understanding of the Law"; Günther Bornkamm, Gerhard Barth, and Heinz Joachim Held, *Tradition and Interpretation in Matthew*. Trans. Percy Scott. London: SCM, 1963.

Barton, Stephen C. "Parables on God's Love and Forgiveness," *The Challenge of Jesus' Parables*, ed. R. N. Longenecker. Grand Rapids/Cambridge, U.K.: Eerdmans, 2000.

Bolt, P. G. "Mark 13: An Apocalyptic Precursor to the Passion Narrative," *Reformed Theological Review* 54 (1995), 48-59.

Brower, K. E. "Blessed are the pure in heart," *Biblical Resources for Holiness Preachers*, vol. 2. Kansas City: Beacon Hill Press of Kansas City, 1995, 15-26.

_____. "Elijah in the Markan Passion Narrative," *Journal for the Study of the New Testament* (JSNT) 18 (1983), 85-101.

_____. "Holiness" in *New Bible Dictionary*, rev. ed. Leicester, U.K.: InterVarsity Press, 1996, 177-178.

_____. "The Holy One and His Disciples: Holiness and Ecclesiology in Mark" in *Holiness and Ecclesiology: Essays on the "Holy Church,"* ed. K. E. Brower and A. Johnson. Grand Rapids: Eerdmans, forthcoming.

_____. "Jesus and the Lustful Eye: Matthew 5:28," *Evangelical Quarterly* (EQ) (2004).

_____. "Let the Reader Understand: Temple and Eschatology in Mark," *Eschatology in Bible and Theology: Evangelical Essays at the Dawn of the New Millennium*, ed. K. E. Brower and M. Elliott. Downers Grove, Ill.: InterVarsity Press, 1997.

_____. "Mark 9:1—Seeing the Kingdom in Power," JSNT 6 (1980), 17-41.

_____. "Re-Minting Christian Holiness." Part 13: "The Parables of Jesus," *The Flame* 66.4 (2000), 7-8.

_____. "Sanctification" in the *New Bible Dictionary*, rev. ed. Leicester, U.K.: InterVarsity Press, 1996, 1057-59.

Davies, G. I. "The Presence of God in the Second Temple and Rabbinic Doctrine," *Templum Amicitiae*, Journal for the Study of the New Testament Supplement Series (JSNTSS) 48; Sheffield: JSOT, 1991.

Drury, Keith. "The Holiness Movement Is Dead," available at http://www.indwes.edu/Tuesday/menu.htm

Dunn, J. D. G. "The Messianic Secret in Mark" in *The Messianic Secret, Issues in Religion and Theology* (IRT) 1, C. M. Tuckett, ed. London/Philadelphia: SCM/Fortress, 1983, 116-31.

_____. "Spirit-and-fire Baptism," *Novum Testamentum* (NovT) 14 (1972), 33-53.

Evans, Craig A. "Jesus and the Continuing Exile of Israel" in *Jesus and the Restoration of Israel,* ed. Carey C. Newman. Carlisle, U.K./Downers Grove, Ill.: Paternoster/ IVP, 1999, 77-100.

Fletcher-Louis, Crispin H. T. "The Destruction of the Temple and the Relativization of the Old Covenant: Mark 13:31 and Matthew 5:18," in Brower and Elliott, *Eschatology in Bible and Theology.*

Head, Peter M. "A Text-Critical Study of Mark 1:1: The Beginning of the Gospel of Jesus Christ," *New Testament Studies* (NTS) 37 (1991), 621-29.

Horbury, W. "Herod's Temple and 'Herod's Days,'" *Templum Amicitiae,* ed. W. Horbury. JSNTSS 48; Sheffield: JSOT, 1991.

Marshall, I. H. "Son of God or Servant of Yahweh?—A Reconsideration of Mark 1:11," NTS 15 (1968-9), 326-36.

Noble, T. A. "1988 Collins Holiness Lectures" (unpublished lectures delivered at Canadian Nazarene College, Winnipeg, Manitoba).

Stibbe, Mark W. G. "The Theology of Renewal and the Renewal of Theology," JPT 3 (1993), 71-90.

Swanson, D. D. "Re-Minting Christian Holiness." Part 8: "Holiness in Leviticus," *The Flame* 66.1 (2000), 17-19.

_____. "Offerings for Sin in Leviticus and John Wesley's Definition," *European Explorations in Christian Holiness* 1 (1999), 9-2.

Thomas, G. J. "A Holy God Among a Holy People in a Holy Place: The Enduring Eschatological Hope," in K. E. Brower and M. W. Elliott, eds., *"The Reader Must Understand": Eschatology in Bible and Theology.* Leicester, U.K.: InterVarsity Press/Apollos, 1997, 53-69. Published in North America as *Eschatology in Bible and Theology: Evangelical Essays at the Dawn of the New Millennium.* Downers Grove, Ill.: IVP, 1999.

## Selected Books

Allison, Dale C. *The New Moses: A Matthean Typology.* Edinburgh: T & T Clark, 1993.

Archer, Léonie J. *Her Price Is Beyond Rubies: The Jewish Woman in Graeco-Roman Palestine,* JSOTS 60. Sheffield, U.K.: JSSOT, 1990.

Bacon, B. W.. *Studies in Matthew.* New York: Holt, 1930.

Barr, James. *Biblical Faith and Natural Theology: The 1991 Gifford Lectures.* Oxford: Oxford University Press, 1995.

_____. *The Semantics of Biblical Language.* Oxford: Oxford University Press, 1961.

Barrett, C. K. *The Holy Spirit and the Gospel Tradition.* London: SPCK, 1947, 1966.

Bauckham, R. J. *God Crucified,* 1996 Didsbury Lectures. Carlisle, U.K.: Paternoster, 1998.

_____. *Jude and the Relatives of Jesus in the Early Church.* Edinburgh: T & T Clark, 1990.

_____, ed. *The Gospel for All Christians: Rethinking the Gospel Audiences.* Edinburgh: T & T Clark, 1998.

Bauckham, Richard, and Trevor Hart. *Hope Against Hope: Christian Eschatology in Contemporary Context.* London: DLT, 1999.

Beasley-Murray, G. R. *Jesus and the Future: An Examination of the Criticism of the Eschatological Discourse, Mark 13 with Special Reference to the Little Apocalypse Theory.* London: Macmillan, 1954.

Betz, H. D. *The Sermon on the Mount: A Commentary on the Sermon on the Mount, Including the Sermon on the Plain. Matthew 5:3—7:27 and Luke 6:20—49.* Hermeneia. Minneapolis: Fortress, 1995.

Borg, Marcus J. *Conflict, Holiness, and Politics in the Teachings of Jesus,* rev. ed. Harrisburg, Pa.: Trinity, 1998; first edition 1984.

Broadhead, Edwin K. *Naming Jesus: Titular Christology in the Gospel of Mark.* JSNTSS 175; Sheffield: SAP, 1999.

Brown, R. E. *The Birth of the Messiah.* New York: Doubleday, 1977.

Bruner, F. D. *The Christbook Matthew 1—12.* Vol. 1 of *Matthew: A Commentary.* Grand Rapids/Carlisle, U.K.: Eerdmans/Paternoster, 2004, rev. and expanded ed.

Bryan, Steven M. *Jesus and Israel's Traditions of Judgement and Restoration.* Society of New Testament Studies, Monograph (SNTSMS) 117. Cambridge, U.K.: Cambridge University Press, 2002.

Caird, G. B., and D. L. Hurst. *New Testament Theology.* Oxford: Clarendon, 1995.

Cunningham, David S. *These Three Are One: The Practice of Trinitarian Theology.* Oxford: Blackwell, 1998.

Davies, W. D., and D. C. Allison. *A Critical and Exegetical Commentary on the Gospel According to Saint Matthew: 1—7.* ICC. Edinburgh: T & T Clark, 1988.

Davies, W. D. *The Setting of the Sermon on the Mount.* Cambridge, U.K.: Cambridge University Press, 1963.

Deasley, A. R. G. *The Shape of Qumran Theology,* 1985 Didsbury Lectures. Carlisle, U.K.: Paternoster, 2000.

Dunn, J. D. G. *The Baptism of the Spirit: A Re-examination of the New Testament Teaching on the Gift of the Spirit in Relation to Pentecostalism Today.* London: SCM, 1970.

_____. *The Partings of the Ways.* London/Harrisburg, Pa.: SCM/Trinity, 1991.

France, R. T. *The Gospel of Mark, New International Greek Testament Commentary* (NIGTC). Grand Rapids/Carlisle, U.K.: Eerdmans/Paternoster, 2002.

_____. *Matthew,* TNTC. Leicester, U.K.: InterVarsity Press, 1985.

_____. *Matthew: Evangelist and Teacher.* Carlisle, U.K.: Paternoster, 1989.

Fredriksen, Paula. *From Jesus to Christ: The Origins of the New Testament Images of Jesus.* New Haven, Conn.: Yale, 1988.

Geddert, T. J. *Watchwords: Mark 13 in Markan Eschatology,* JSNTSS 26. Sheffield, U.K.: JSOT, 1989.

Gerhardsson, Birger. *The Testing of God's Son. Matt. 4:1—11 and Parallels,* Coniectanea Biblica, New Testament Series (ConBNT) 2.1. Lund, Swed.: Gleerup, 1966.

Greathouse, William M. *Wholeness in Christ: Toward a Biblical Theology of Holiness.* Kansas City: Beacon Hill Press of Kansas City, 1998.

Green, Joel B. *The Gospel of Luke,* NICNT. Grand Rapids/Carlisle, U.K.: Eerdmans/Paternoster, 1997.

_____. *The Theology of the Gospel of Luke.* New Testament Theology. Cambridge, U.K.: Cambridge University Press, 1995.

Guelich, Robert A. *The Sermon on the Mount.* Waco, Tex.: Word, 1982.

Gundry, R. H. *A Commentary on His Apology for the Cross.* Grand Rapids: Eerdmans, 1993.

_____. *The Use of the Old Testament in St. Matthew's Gospel, Supplements to Novum Testamentum* (NovTSup) 18. Leiden, Neth.: E. J. Brill, 1967.

Gunton, Colin E. *Christ and Creation,* 1990 Didsbury Lectures. Carlisle, U.K.: Paternoster, 1993.

_____. *The Promise of Trinitarian Theology,* 2nd ed. Edinburgh: T & T Clark, 1997.

_____. *The Triune Creator.* Edinburgh: Edinburgh University Press, 1998.

Hagner, Donald A. *Matthew 1—13,* WBC 33A. Dallas: Word, 1993.

Harrington, Hannah. *Holiness: Rabbinic Judaism and the Graeco-Roman World.* London/New York: Routledge, 2001.

Hartley, John E. *Leviticus,* WBC 4. Dallas: Word, 1995.

Hengel, Martin, and Anna Maria Schwemer. *Paul Between Damascus and Antioch.* Trans. John Bowden. London: SCM, 1997.

Hooker, M. D. *Continuity and Discontinuity.* London: Epworth, 1986.

Hurtado, L. W. *At the Origins of Christian Worship,* 1999 Didsbury Lectures. Carlisle, U.K.: Paternoster, 2000.

_____. *Lord Jesus Christ: Devotion to Jesus in Earliest Christianity.* Grand Rapids: Cambridge, U.K.: Eerdmans, 2003.

_____. *One God, One Lord.* Edinburgh: T & T Clark, 1998, rev. of the original 1980 ed.

Jenson, Philip. *Graded Holiness: A Key to the Priestly Conception of the World.* JSOTSS 106; Sheffield: SAP, 1993.

Keener, Craig S. *A Commentary on the Gospel of Matthew.* Grand Rapids/Cambridge, U.K.: Eerdmans, 1990.

Kingsbury, J. D. *Matthew.* 3d ed. Nappanee, Ind.: Evangel, 1998.

Kissinger, W. S. *The Sermon on the Mount: A History of Interpretation and Bibliography.* Metuchen, N.J.: Scarecrow, 1975.

Kruse, Colin G. *John* in TNTC. Leicester, U.K./Grand Rapids: InterVarsity Press/Eerdmans, 2003/2004.

Kupp, David D. *Matthew's Emmanuel: Divine Presence and God's People in the First Gospel,* SNTSMS 90. Cambridge, U.K.: Cambridge University Press, 1996.

Lightfoot, R. H. *The Gospel Message of St. Mark.* Oxford: Oxford University Press, 1950.

Lodahl, Michael. *The Story of God.* Kansas City: Beacon Hill Press of Kansas City, 1997.

Luz, Ulrich. *Matthew 1—7: A Commentary.* Trans. W. C. Linss; Minneapolis/Edinburgh: Augsburg Fortress/T & T Clark, 1989/1990.

_____. *The Theology of the Gospel of Matthew,* New Testament Theology Series (NTT). Trans. J. Bradford Robinson. Cambridge, U.K.: Cambridge University Press, 1995.

Marcus, Joel. *The Way of the Lord: Christological Exegesis of the Old Testament in the Gospel of Mark.* Edinburgh: T & T Clark, 1993.

Marxsen, W. *Mark the Evangelist: Studies on the Redaction History of the Gospel.* Trans. Roy A. Harrisville, et al. Nashville/New York: Abingdon, 1969.

Mauser, Ulrich. *Christ in the Wilderness: The Wilderness Theme in the Second Gospel and Its Basis in the Biblical Tradition,* Studies in Biblical Theology (SBT) 39. London: SCM, 1963.

McFarlane, Graham. *Christ and the Spirit: The Doctrine of the Incarnation According to Edward Irving.* Carlisle, U.K.: Paternoster, 1996.

McGrath, Alister. *Understanding the Trinity.* Eastbourne, U.K.: Kingsway, 1986.

McKnight, Scot. *A New Vision for Israel: The Teachings of Jesus in National Context.* Grand Rapids: Eerdmans, 1999.

Menzies, R. P. *Empowered for Witness: The Spirit in Luke-Acts.* Sheffield, U.K.: SAP, 1994.

Meyer, Ben F. *The Aims of Jesus.* London: SCM, 1979.

Nolland, J. *Luke 1—9:20. Word Biblical Commentary* (WBC) 35A. Dallas: Word, 1989.

Otto, Rudolf. *The Idea of the Holy.* Trans. John W. Harvey. Oxford: Oxford University Press, 1923.

Peterson, David. *Possessed by God: A New Testament Theology of Sanctification and Holiness.* Leicester, U.K.: InterVarsity Press/Apollos, 1995.

Pinnock, Clark D. *The Flame of Love.* Downers Grove, Ill.: InterVarsity Press, 1998.

_____ and Robert C. Brow. *Unbounded Love.* Carlisle, U.K.: Paternoster, 1994.

Powell, M. A. *Jesus as a Figure in History: How Modern Historians View the Man from Galilee.* Louisville, Ky.: Westminster/John Knox, 1998.

Powell, Samuel M. *Holiness in the 21st Century: Call, Consecration, and Obedience Perfected in Love.* San Diego: Point Loma Press, 2004.

Purkiser, W. T. *Exploring Christian Holiness.* Vol. 1, *Biblical Foundations.* Kansas City: Beacon Hill Press of Kansas City, 1983.

Quanstrom, Mark R. *A Century of Holiness Theology: The Doctrine of Entire Sanctification in the Church of the Nazarene: 1905 to 2004.* Kansas City: Beacon Hill Press of Kansas City, 2004.

Robinson, J. A. T. *The Priority of John.* London: SCM, 1985.

Sanders, E. P. *Jesus and Judaism.* London: SCM, 1985.

_____. *Paul and Palestinian Judaism.* London: SCM, 1977.

Seutonius. *Life of Claudius* 25.4.

Stendahl, Krister. *The School of St. Matthew and Its Use of the Old Testament,* rev. ed. Philadelphia: Fortress, 1968.

Strecker, Georg. *The Sermon on the Mount: An Exegetical Commentary.* Trans. O. C. Dean Jr. Nashville: Abingdon, 1988.

Stronstad, Roger. *The Charismatic Theology of St. Luke.* Peabody, Mass.: Hendrickson, 1984.

Swartley, Willard. *Mark: The Way for All Nations.* Scottdale, Pa.: Herald, 1981.

Turner, M. M. B. *The Holy Spirit and Spiritual Gifts Then and Now.* Carlisle, U.K.: Paternoster, 1996.

_____. *Power from On High.* Sheffield, U.K.: SAP, 1996.

Volf, Miroslav. *After Our Likeness: The Church as the Image of the Trinity,* Sacra Doctrina. Grand Rapids/Cambridge, U.K.: Eerdmans, 1998.

Ware, Kallistos. *The Orthodox Way.* London: Mowbray, 1979.

Ware, Timothy (Kallistos). *The Orthodox Church.* London: Penguin, 1993 [rev. ed.].

Watts, Rikki E. *Isaiah's New Exodus and Mark*. Tübingen: J. C. B. Mohr/Paul Siebeck, 1997.

Webber, Robert E. *Evangelicals on the Canterbury Trail*. London: Moorhouse, 1989.

Wenham, David. *The Rediscovery of Jesus' Eschatological Discourse, Gospel Perspectives* 4. Sheffield, U.K.: JSOT, 1984.

Wenham, Gordon J. *Genesis 1—15*, WBC 1. Waco, Tex.: Word, 1987.

Williamson, H. G. M. *Variations on a Theme: King, Messiah and Servant in the Book of Isaiah*, 1997 Didsbury Lectures. Carlisle, U.K.: Paternoster, 1998.

Wink, Walter. *Naming the Powers: The Language of Power in the New Testament; Unmasking the Powers: Forces That Determine Human Existence; and Engaging the Powers: Discernment and Resistance in a World of Domination*. Philadelphia: Fortress, 1984, 1986, 1992.

_____. *When the Powers Fail: Reconciliation Among the Nations*. Minneapolis: Fortress Augsburg, 1998.

Wright, G. E. *The Acts of God: Biblical Theology as Recital*, SBT 8. London: SCM, 1952.

Wright, N. T. *Jesus and the Victory of God*. Vol. 2 of *Christian Origins and the Question of God*. London: SPCK, 1993.

_____. *The New Testament and the People of God*. Vol. 1 of *Christian Origins and the Question of God*. London: SPCK, 1992.

Wynkoop, Mildred Bangs. *A Theology of Love: The Dynamic of Wesleyanism*. Kansas City: Beacon Hill Press of Kansas City, 1972.

Yuill, Chick. *We Need Saints*. London: Salvation Army, 1998, rev.

Ziesler, J. A. *The Meaning of Righteousness in Paul: A Linguistic and Theological Enquiry*, SNTSMS 20. Cambridge, U.K.: Cambridge University Press, 1972.

Zizioulas, John D. *Being as Communion: Studies in Personhood and the Church*. Crestwood: St. Vladimir's Seminary Press, 1993.

*did not get past pg 4/5 = not very interesting*

*ok maybe for the sem grad working on a Ph.D.*

# Guide to Forgiveness Meditation

*An Effective Method to Dissolve Blocks to Loving-Kindness and Living in the Present*

Bhante Vimalaramsi

Other Books by Bhante Vimalaramsi:


*A Guide to Tranquil Wisdom Insight Meditation*   2016

*Meditation is Life, Life is Meditation*             2014

*The Dhamma Leaf Series*                             2014

*Moving Dhamma Vol 1.*                               2012

*Breath of Love*                                     2011

*Anapanasati Sutta*                             1998-2003

*"There is no question that Forgiveness Meditation is part of Loving-Kindness Meditation development.*

*It is the first step towards Peace."*

# Table of Contents

## Acknowledgement

This booklet was based on a talk I gave in 2012 at DSMC. It was done with the intention of making a video for the internet concerning my basic technique of working with Forgiveness in meditation. This talk is on our web site.

I wish to acknowledge Ven. Sister Khema's hard work in transcribing this talk, for seeing and conceiving a potential book, for her primary editing, and offering her own additions and advice during final editing. I also wish to thank a dearly departed Dhamma supporter, Dr. Otha Wingo for his contributions in helping to improve the clarity of this subject into a format for easier reading. This was a great contribution for us all. And David for final editing and publishing in book form.

# *Foreword*

When Ven. Sister Khema requested me to write a forward to this booklet I accepted the invitation with considerable pleasure since I esteem being associated with this literary endeavor of unusual significance and immense practical relevance.

It is common knowledge that a large number of books and other literary works have been published on the subject of all aspects of meditative practices leading to 'Loving Kindness Meditation'. The less discerning public might wonder 'why another booklet on the same subject'. The author perhaps anticipating such hesitation and misgiving has stated the principal objective of this booklet in very clear and precise terms. Without being far too exhaustive, highly specialized or too scholarly to be of much practical help to the uninstructed and uninitiated or even to the average person seeking basic concise guidance, the author has provided us a brief, clear and simple handbook which is a much-felt need. Even a cursory glance of the booklet should make it clear that this booklet is an entirely fresh orchestration of most of the salient issues of Forgiveness Meditation.

Often the author's language is unusually illustrative. For instance here is a classic example: "....we can clear the runway for our Mindfulness of Loving-Kindness to take off by first learning to use Mindfulness of Forgiveness meditation. This is an extremely powerful cleansing practice." (Page 8)

The Buddha's supreme and timeless proclamation of liberation of thought and the prioritization of the mind over twenty-five centuries ago is now universally accepted by modern day scientists. As humanity advances and with intellectual development, the quest for spiritual solace enhances this advancement. The author clearly indicates the principal and unique feature of the discipline of the mind through meditation.

This booklet shows in clear and simple terms the way towards spiritual cleansing and dispelling psychic irritants. A commendable feature of this booklet is that the treatment is basic but very precise and comprehensive. I have no doubt whatsoever that this booklet will help the readers towards meaningful practice of 'Forgiveness Meditation' leading to the successful practice of 'Loving-Kindness Meditation'.

*"Bhavatu Sabba Maṅgalaṃ !"*
May you have All Good Blessings!

Ven. H. Kondañña, Abbot
Staten Island Buddhist Vihara

# Introduction

The Buddha was a meditation teacher. He taught meditation for 45 years after he became fully awakened. When you study and practice meditation you will not be entirely successful until you master the definitions and interwoven nature of two words. Meditation and Mindfulness. I can give you the definitions but then you must experience for yourself how these two work together.

In the Buddhist teachings, Meditation means, 'observing the movement of mind's attention moment-to-moment, in order to see clearly how the links Dependent Origination actually work.' Mindfulness means 'remembering to observe '<u>How</u>' mind's attention moves from one thing to another. This use of mindfulness actually causes mind to become sharper as you go as you experience more subtle states of mind. It isn't hard to see why you must develop this precise mindfulness to keep the meditation going smoothly.

Many people practice Loving-Kindness meditation, but, according to a few people, the power of it doesn't seem to change much for them in their daily lives. If it doesn't take off quite right in the beginning, we might run into difficulty with this practice and it can be like hitting a wall. It's good to know that there is a key to the solution for developing metta in our daily activities. That solution is learning to smile as much as you can remember.

Apparently, in some cases, if we do get into trouble, we can clear the runway for our Mindfulness of Loving-Kindness to take off by first learning to use Mindfulness of Forgiveness meditation.  This is an extremely powerful and cleansing practice. Forgiveness is a form of loving-kindness that really clears our mind of negative or unwholesome states.

The reason this book came into being is because of the many questions teachers are asked about 'why doesn't my Mettā arise easily?'.  It is because we need to forgive ourselves first before we can send out pure love to others.

# CHAPTER ONE - Preparation

**At times,** there can be confusion about how to effectively practice this Mindfulness of Forgiveness meditation. So, this booklet is dedicated only to this meditation on forgiveness so you can begin the practice with a clear goal and better understanding.

When people are practicing Loving-Kindness Meditation, you might run into a barrier as you try to send out Loving-Kindness to yourself and to others. If this happens after a few days, and you are not successful in feeling the metta in the retreat, it may be suggested for you to take a step back and start doing the Forgiveness Meditation to overcome these blocks. After all, we cannot sincerely send Loving-kindness and Forgiveness to someone else when we do not have it for ourselves. This practice is not just used for a person pursuing Loving-Kindness and Compassion meditation. Any person can make the commitment to clean house by doing this forgiveness work. After this is done for the first time, one feels many years younger, because often times, a great weight has been lifted off your heart and mind.

Some people have the idea that this meditation is a completely different kind of meditation from the Loving-

Kindness meditation. That is not so. It should be made clear from the beginning that the Forgiveness Meditation is not outside of the development of Loving-Kindness and is a part of metta. For anyone who has difficulty in feeling loving-kindness, this can be the first step. It creates a firm bridge between heart and mind that is then used to help all other kinds of meditation succeed. It is a cleansing for the heart: another opening of the heart we can add to our initial practice of Generosity.

In truth, this meditation is probably the most powerful meditation that I know. It can clear away mental blocks that pop up from old attachments or dislikes towards various people, or events that happened to you in your past life experiences. If you follow directions closely, and you are patient when you practice, then pain and suffering will gradually dissolve any hard-heartedness you still carry in your mind, about past life wounds.

When you practice Forgiveness meditation, all of the basic rules will remain the same. You still sit in a reasonably quiet space to do this work. Be sure you are wearing loose comfortable clothing. Sit in a comfortable position, on the floor or in a chair. If you do use a chair, don't lean into the back of the chair. Sit with your spine nicely straight but not tightly erect. Sit in a position that does not bring up physical pain in general for you. You should follow the basics of practicing Right Effort using Tranquil Wisdom Insight Meditation (TWIM) and the 6Rs for your meditation cycle to accomplish your goal.

When you practice, sit for a minimum of 30 minutes each time. Sit longer if things are going smoothly and you have the time. At whatever time you decide to break your sitting, stand up slowly. Keep your observation going as you stand up. Stretch slowly if desired.

While you are sitting, do not move at all. Don't wiggle your toes, don't scratch. If your body needs to cough or sneeze, do not hold this in; just sneeze or cough! Keep some tissues close by for any tears that might arise. If tears do fall, then let them come. That is what you have holes in your eyelids for... So, let the tears come out. This releases the pressure. Consider this the cleansing time before you take up any other primary meditations.

While practicing Forgiveness meditation, please use ONLY these meditation instructions and put all other meditation instructions aside until you have completed the work. This just means that we don't want to confuse mind, so, don't mix up the recipe! We want only the information needed to do this practice.

# CHAPTER TWO - Instructions

**The way you start** practicing forgiveness meditation is by forgiving yourself.

There are different kinds of statements that you can use for this to help bring up any old grudges and hard-heartedness locked inside you. You may pick one statement to begin and then you stay with that statement for a period of time, to give it a chance to settle in and you and see what comes up. The first suggested phrase is **"I forgive myself for not understanding."** Everybody has misunderstandings that happen in their life. Nobody is exempt from this fact.

**While you are sitting** you repeat the phrase, "I forgive myself for not understanding". After you've done that, you put that feeling into your heart and stay with that feeling of forgiveness. When that feeling fades away or the mind gets distracted, then you come back and forgive yourself for not understanding again. If you are familiar with the 6R process you should 6R any distractions arise. The appendix has a large section on how you practice the 6Rs.

For those familiar with the Jhanas, and have meditated before, it is necessary to not go higher than the first jhana.

You can't mentally verbalize beyond that (say your phrases for forgiveness). Please make a determination to not go any deeper. This is an active contemplative process that we are doing now.

While you're doing this, your mind is going to have some resistance to this meditation. Your mind is going to take off and say, "Well, this is stupid! I shouldn't be doing this! Reactions like these are part of your attachments. These are the obstacles that we must dissolve.

Stay with your statement and repeat, "I forgive myself for not understanding".  Then your mind might say, "AAH! I don't need to do this anymore. This meditation doesn't work". Every thought that pulls you away from forgiving yourself for not understanding is an attachment and has to be let go and the tension and tightness in that attachment must be "relaxed" away.

This is where you use the 6R's you learned with your basic Metta meditation practice. The 6R's are Recognize< Release < Relax < Re-Smile > Return > Repeat. That is the entire cycle.  You RECOGNIZE that mind is distracted. You RELEASE the distraction by not keeping your attention on it.  You RELAX the tightness in your head and heart and you RE-SMILE; and then you softly come back to the statement and you stay with the statement for as long as you can. If you are distracted again you repeat the process.

It doesn't matter how many times your mind gets distracted. One thing that many people get caught with is getting wrapped up in the story about things and this can

cause lots of pain and suffering along with some frustration. The 6R's will help you to see how strong the attachments are and it shows the way to overcome the suffering they cause. Recognize it. Let it be. Relax. Smile. Come back and stay with the feeling of forgiveness for as long as you can.

Sitting should be followed by Walking Practice. If you are going to continue sitting again, or you are going to return to a task in daily life, before you do, take a stroll, at a normal pace to keep your blood flowing nicely. Walk for about 15 minutes minimum in some fresh air. 45 minutes is a good maximum time for walking. If you are working in a restricted space setting, find a space that is level and at least 30 feet long in length. Walk back and forth, and mentally, keep your meditation going.

**\*When you walk** you want to walk in a way that you repeat the phrases with each stride as you walk. Like this - with the left foot take a step and mentally say **"I"** then a right step **"forgive"** and left say **"you"**. Then again, but say, **"You"** on the right step, and then left step, **"forgive"**, right step, **"me"**. And repeat. Back and forth. It can get into a nice cadence but all the while it is really getting it into your 'noggin' to forgive! "I forgive you, you forgive me". And keep smiling when you are doing this. And 6R anything or anyone who comes up. Stay with the walking. I used to go for 6-8 mile walks in Hawaii doing just this practice!

The idea of sitting and walking is to create a continuous flow of meditation without stopping. This proves you can keep the meditation with you all the time in life. While

walking at this normal pace, continue doing the forgiveness meditation with your eyes looking down towards the ground about 6 or 7 feet in front of you. Do not look around. Keep on gently forgiving. Keep smiling all the time.

# CHAPTER THREE - Attachments

One mistake that an awful lot of people make is they say, "Well, meditation is just for sitting. The rest of the time I don't have anything else to do, so, I can let my mind act like it always does." This is a mistake. We need to consider the idea that Meditation is life and Life is meditation. You want to realize that you have attachments in your daily life and just because you are not sitting doesn't mean those attachments aren't there. The whole point in doing the meditation is for personality development. It's for letting go of old habitual suffering [bhava}, and in place of this, developing a mind that has equanimity in it.

The more resistance your mind has in doing this, the more you need to do it, because the resistance is your mind showing you where your attachment is, and that is the cause of suffering. This meditation works better than anything that I know of for letting go of attachments, letting go and relaxing of old hard-hearted feelings [bhava], letting go of the way you think the world is supposed to be, so you can start accepting the way the world actually is.

Your mind might say, "Well, I don't like that! I don't like the way they said this or that." Ask yourself now, "Who doesn't like it? Who is judging and condemning? Who is

making up a story? Who is caught by their attachment?"
"Well, 'I' am!"

It might be helpful here to give a definition of attachment. An attachment is anything we take personally, any thought, any feeling, any sensation! When we think these thoughts or feelings are "mine", this is "me", this is who "I" am, at that point, mind has become attached and this causes craving to arise in your mind and body.

Craving always manifests as a tension or tightness in both mind and body. Craving is the "I" like it, "I" don't like it mind - which arises in everyone's mind/body process. Attachment is another word for craving and is the start of all suffering. When we see that everything that arises is part of an impersonal process, then, we begin to understand what it is like to see things with a clear observant mind.

Somebody might say something very innocently and you hear it through your attachment and it's negative. This is why we have to learn how to become aware of what is happening all the time in our daily lives.

When you get finished sitting in your meditation for 30 minutes, 45 minutes, or for an hour and you start walking around, what does your mind do? It takes off just like it always does. It thinks about this. It thinks about that. This is just non-sense thoughts.

Most of us think those thoughts and those feelings that arise are ours personally; that they are not just random things. But, in truth, if you feed any kind of a thought or feeling with your attention, you make it bigger and more

intense. When you realize that you are causing your own suffering, you have to forgive yourself for doing that.

This means saying, "I forgive myself for not understanding. I forgive myself completely." Of course, your mind is going to take off again and say,"Aah! This is stupid! This is nothing. This isn't real. This isn't what is actually happening. 'I' don't want to do this!"

Every one of those thoughts is an attachment, isn't it? Every one of those thoughts has craving in it, doesn't it? Every one of those thoughts is causing you suffering, right?

Because of this, you have to recognize that you are doing this to yourself and let go of those thoughts. That's just nonsense stuff anyway. It doesn't have anything to do with what you are doing and where you are right now. Once you know this, you forgive yourself for not understanding; for causing yourself pain; for causing other people pain. YOU REALLY FORGIVE.

Take a look at when you are walking from here to there. What are you doing with your mind? "Ho Hum. Thinking about this, and, I gotta do that, and, I have to go talk to that person, and, I have to do this." All of that's non-sense!

Now, this doesn't mean that you can't plan what you need to do next. You can. But just do that planning one time as your primary topic in the present moment. After you make up your mind what the plan is, you don't have to think about it anymore. Repeating it, rolling it around again; all of that is just part of your old habitual tendency (bhava in Pāli). It

is your old conditioned thoughts and feelings, and taking them personally and causing yourself pain and suffering.

# CHAPTER FOUR - Daily Practice

Including the exercise of forgiveness in your daily activity is by far the most important part of this meditation. You forgive yourself continually, for not understanding, for getting caught up in this or that, for taking things personally. How many times have you found yourself doing this? "Hey! I don't like the way you said that." Ask yourself. WHO doesn't like what? "Well, you said something that was hurtful." To WHOM?

You need to stop and realize that you're taking all this stuff personally and it's not really personal. It's just stuff that happens. Forgive it! Forgive it even when you're walking along a road and you happen to kick a rock and it hurts. Forgive the pain for being there! Your job is to keep your mind forgiving all the time. That's what Mindfulness of Forgiveness Meditation practice is all about. The technique is not just about when you are sitting. This is a life practice. This is an all-the-time practice.

If you want to really begin to change, you have to be willing to go through the forgiveness sincerely, because it will help you change a lot. You have to have patience and it helps to have a sense of humor about just how dumb mind

can be.  The more you smile and laugh the easier the meditation becomes.

# CHAPTER FIVE - Finding Balance

Whenever you personally continue to think about this and that, to judge this and condemn that, you are constantly causing yourself suffering. You don't need to do that. You want to argue with other people about your attachments? What's the point? When you really start practicing forgiveness for yourself, or forgiveness for another person, your mind starts to get into balance and your sense of humor begins to change. This is equanimity. Then you don't take thoughts, feelings and sensations and all this other stuff personally.

When you practice in this way, you are seeing life for what it is and allowing it to be there. It's not worth going over it in your mind, and over it, and over it, and over it. It's not worth it. It's a waste of time. It's a waste of effort. Every time you have a repeat thought, you are attached. You're identifying with that thought and you're taking it personally and that is again the cause of suffering. What you are seeing here is the Second Noble Truth. You are witnessing how Craving, taking it personally is the cause of suffering. And you can't blame anybody else for it. It's yours. You are doing it all to yourself. "WELL, they said this!"

So what?

Others may have their opinion. That doesn't mean 'I' have to listen to them. I don't have to take it in personally and analyze whether it's correct or not, because it doesn't matter. The more you forgive in your daily life and daily activities, the easier it is to forgive the big things that happened in the past.

# CHAPTER SIX - Persistence

When you're doing the Forgiveness Meditation while you're sitting, you're staying with one of the suggested statements. You stay with that one statement until you internally feel, "YES, I really do forgive myself for not understanding." It's important to work this through.

To really forgive can take awhile. It's not just some quick fix to do in one sitting and then you come in and say, "OK, now I'm done!", or you say, "I've already done that". Doing that is not where you're going to get real change. Nope. You still have your attachments there. You still have to continually forgive yourself for not understanding, forgive yourself for making a mistake. That is what not understanding is about. You have to forgive yourself for judging, for condemning, for analyzing, for thinking, for getting angry. Forgive everything, all of the time.

When I started to do the forgiveness meditation, which, I did personally for myself for two years, because I wanted to make sure I really understood this meditation, I went through major changes. There were major changes; major personality changes. If you want that for yourself, you have to have that kind of patience.

This idea of, "Well, I've already forgiven this person or that person", that simply isn't it. A little later on you figure out that you're talking about how YOU didn't like this or that from them! Ah! Guess what? Who hasn't finished their forgiveness meditation? YOU haven't forgiven yourself, or that other person!

# CHAPTER SEVEN - *Going Deeper*

When you start to go deeper in your meditation, staying with the forgiveness, and you do forgive yourself for making mistakes, there can come a time when somebody comes up into your mind that you need to forgive.

When this happens, you realize that you did not ask them to come up. You do not stop and say, "Well, I need this person to come up." They came up by themselves.

As soon as that person comes up, you start forgiving them, for not understanding. It doesn't matter what they did in the past. All of your thoughts, all of your opinions of what they did in the past just keep bringing up more suffering.

These thoughts come up because of your attachment. "I didn't like that! I didn't want that to happen! They are a dirty no good so and so because they did that to me." Can you guess where the attachment is? Guess where the idea comes from that I can blame somebody else for my own suffering? The only person you can blame for your suffering is yourself. Why? Because, YOU are the one that took it personally. You're the one who had an opinion about it. You're the one that used your habitual tendencies

over and over again to justify the idea that I'm right and you're wrong. That's how we cause our own suffering.

The forgiveness meditation helps you let go of that opinion, that idea, that attachment, and feel some relief. Because some past person did or said something that caused anger, resentment, jealousy, pain or whatever the catch of the day was – it can have a real tendency for your mind to get caught up in thinking about that past event.

This is called getting caught by the story. You need to use the 6R's and then go back to your forgiveness statement. It doesn't matter how many times the story arises, please use the 6R's and then forgive again. The story's emotion will fade away after you do this enough. This is where patience is needed.

# CHAPTER EIGHT - Letting Go

When you see someone else come up in your mind, somebody you really had a rough time with and you didn't like it; someone you started hating for whatever reason, you forgive them. With your mind's eye, you look them straight in their eye and you tell them sincerely: "I forgive you for not understanding the situation, I forgive you for causing me pain, I forgive you completely."

Now, keep that person in your heart and radiate Forgiveness to them. If your mind has a distraction and it pulls you away from that; you might hear in your mind, "No, I don't, that no good so and so. I won't forgive him!" Using the 6R's, let go of this and come back and say, "I do forgive you."

It has to be sincere. "Well, I'm not going to forgive that dirty no good so and so." Why not? "Because, they caused 'ME' suffering!" Oops! WHO caused who suffering? YOU caused your own self suffering because you took it personally, and YOU reinforced that with a lot of thoughts and opinions and ideas about why that was wrong.

In other words, you were caught in your craving, your own clinging, your habitual tendencies and that leads to more and more dissatisfaction, aversion, pain and suffering.

# CHAPTER NINE - Relief

It's really important to realize that this is not an easy practice. It's hard to forgive someone when they have really caused you harm. Take a woman that has been raped or a man who has been beaten and robbed. It's hard to forgive the person who raped them or beat them because they have been violated. But, holding onto their hatred of that person is keeping them attached. It doesn't matter what the action was. It doesn't matter what happened in the past. What matters is what you are doing with what you have in your mind right now.

To completely develop this practice to the highest level means that you keep forgiving and forgiving! Over and over. With your mind's eye, you look them straight in the eye and you say, "I really do forgive you." And your mind says, "NO, I DON'T" And you let that go, and 6R, and come back. You say, "I really do forgive you." Then take that person and put them in your heart and continue to radiate forgiveness to them. How long do you do that? As long as it takes.

For some attachments, one or two sittings is all you will need. Some other attachments, might take a week; might take two weeks or even longer. Who knows? It doesn't

matter. If you need time, you can take time! You have all the time there is.


You will feel a very, very strong sense of relief when you let go of the hatred you have towards these people. Then any time you think of them, you kind of think of them with a mind that says, "Well, they made a mistake, they didn't know what they were doing. It's ok."

That's how you let go of an attachment (craving). That's how you let go of the pain of that past situation. This doesn't mean that the person who was violated is going to go up and hug the person who did that to them. They would avoid them because they know there is a possibility of personal harm. But they don't hate them anymore. They don't think about it anymore. They have let it go.

That's what the forgiveness is all about. It's about letting go. You are giving up old dissatisfaction and dislike. You are developing a mind that says, "Well that's ok. You can be like that." That is not taking it personally.

# CHAPTER TEN - Obstacles

The biggest part of the Mindfulness of Forgiveness Meditation is learning how to let go of your personal opinions, ideas, concepts, stories. You might stay with a person for a long period of time because of your opinions and your attachment to this.

Every time you are doing any walking or sitting meditation, keep forgiving them over and over again. Your mind might get bored with that and say, "OH, I don't want to do this anymore!"

Well that's another kind of attachment, isn't it? So, what do you do with that? You have to get through it by forgiving the boredom for being there. That's ok. Your mind is tricky. It's going to try to distract you any way it can. It'll bring up any kind of feelings and thoughts and ideas to distract you, because, it doesn't like the idea of giving up attachments. Your mind really feels comfortable, holding onto attachments.

We need to go easy on ourselves as we develop this practice. After all, how many years did it take us to build up our habits [bhava]? It takes patience to move in the opposite direction now and to change those unwholesome

mind-states into new wholesome tendencies. Be kind to yourself and take your time.

The whole point of the Meditation is LEARNING HOW TO CHANGE. Learning how to let go of those old non-sense ideas and thoughts and develop new ideas and thoughts that make you happy and make other people around you happy too. That's the whole reason for the precepts. They outline an option for us to follow so we gain balance in our life.

Let's take a quick look at the precepts. Do not kill any living beings on purpose. Don't take what is not freely given to you (no stealing). Don't engage in wrong sexual activity with another person's mate or a person too young living with their parents. In short, don't do anything that will cause mental or physical harm to any other human being. Don't engage in telling lies, using harsh language, gossip, or slander. Lastly, don't take recreational drugs or alcohol because these will weaken mind and the tendency to break the other precepts is stronger!

These precepts are like an ultimate operational manual for life. If you keep them well, then you get the most out of your life, they make you, and others around you happy. The more you can continually follow them, the better your frame of mind will become. You will more easily forgive that other person, your mind will become softer towards that person, and you will feel more relief.

What happens is, after you practice this way for a while, then you go "Ah, I do, I really do forgive you!" and there's no, energy behind it at all. It's just like, "yeah, this

happened; it's in the past; it's no big deal." This is what forgiveness is all about.

# CHAPTER ELEVEN - Daily Life

How can this practice affect your daily life?  This is a good question.   You're more open, you're more accepting.  You're not judging.  You're not condemning.  You're not dis- liking, because as you see that tightness of mind coming up in you, and you go, "Oops! I forgive you for not understanding this one!", and you smile.  You let it go.

One of the hardest things a guiding teacher has to do is to teach people that 'Life is supposed to be fun'.  It's a game!  Keep it light!  If you, play with your mind and your attachments that means you are not being attached to them so much.  As you play with them, you're not taking them so seriously anymore.  When you don't take them seriously, they're easier to let go of.

That's what the Buddha was teaching us!  He was teaching us how to have an uplifted mind all of the time; how to be able to be light with your thoughts, with your feelings, and your ideas, and your past actions.

Yes.  It's true.  On some occasion you made a mistake.  Well? Ok!  Welcome to the human race!  I don't know of anyone who hasn't made a mistake and felt guilty about it.  Sure they do.

And what is that guilt? Non-forgiveness. That's an example of your mind grabbing onto what's happening and saying, "I really screwed up and I need to punish myself for that." That's what your mind is saying. Now do you see what you can do about this? Right! The more you become serious with your daily life, the more attachments you will have. The less equanimity, the less mental balance you will have in your life.

There is no question about it. You're on these roller coasters; emotional roller coasters, up and down, up and down, up and down. When you start forgiving more, those high high's, and low low's start to turn into little waves. You still have some. But you don't get caught for as long. You just stop and say, "This just isn't important enough to get upset about."

# CHAPTER TWELVE - *Success!*

After you forgive that person, you stay with them; you stay with that person that's come up into your mind until you feel like, "Enough! I don't have to do this anymore. I really have forgiven you." At that point, with your mind's eye, you look them straight in the eye, and you stop verbalizing and you hear them say back to you: "I forgive you too."

Wow! Now this is different, isn't it? It's kind of remarkable. You have this feeling of being forgiven as well as you forgiving them! You've forgiven yourself for making mistakes, for not understanding. You've forgiven that other person for making mistakes, for not understanding, or causing pain, whatever you want using the statement that really makes it true for you. And, now, you hear them say "I forgive you."

There is a real sense of relief. Wow! What happens in your mind now is that JOY comes up in your mind. You feel light. You feel really happy. Happier then you ever felt before. You didn't realize you were carrying these big bundles of rocks on your shoulders, holding you down, did you? And now, you have put them down. When you forgive,

the heaviness of those hard feelings and "rocks" disappear. You feel light. "Oh My! This REALLY is great stuff!"

It takes a lot of work, but, it's worth it. It's not easy. Why isn't it easy? Because of the amount of attachment we have when we begin. You keep doing the meditation and when you get done with one person, you go back to yourself. You repeat: "I forgive myself for making mistakes. I forgive myself for not understanding." You stay with yourself until somebody else comes up into your mind. You keep on doing that until your mind says, "OK. I've done it. Everything is good. There's nobody else. Enough!"

At this time, you can switch back to your Mindfulness of Loving-Kindness meditation and make it your primary formal practice. Now you can understand why Mindfulness of Forgiveness Meditation is definitely part of Loving-Kindness. How can you ever practice Loving-Kindness if you have hatred? You can't. This practice releases the Hatred.

# CHAPTER THIRTEEN – Not Easy

This practice has NO simple, easy, fast-fix here! You can't just buy the solution this time at the Mall either. You have to patiently continue this practice all the time until you release the unwholesome mind-states which are your old habitual tendencies of mind.

Depending how attached you are to the idea that a person wronged you, or the idea of how badly you screwed up, this leads you into "I can never forgive myself." Until you finally go through this process of forgiveness, you will not be free of this burden.

You WILL know when you have gone entirely through the Mindfulness of Forgiveness Meditation because then you will be free and you will see clearly this is how Forgiveness really works. Are you done? You don't have to have anybody to tell you that this worked. You'll know!

The daily continuous work of this practice is most important. When you are walking from one place to another, I don't care what you are doing. Any kind of distraction that comes up, forgive it. Smile. If a person comes up to you and they start talking and you don't want to talk, FORGIVE THEM. They don't understand. They don't

understand what you are doing. It's ok that they don't understand. It's ok that they don't know where you are or what you are doing. They can judge you, they can condemn you, they can cause all kinds of distractions, and that's fine. They can do that. BUT, as for you, you can forgive them for it.

As you are forgiving them, you are letting go of the attachment to the way 'I' think things are supposed to be. Not understanding can be a really big thing. Because we don't understand so much; we have our own opinions and ideas of the way things are supposed to work; that can be a problem. We get caught up by assumption. That's it, isn't it?

What happens when things don't match your idea of the way things are supposed to work? What then? You may find yourself fighting with REALITY which is the truth, the Dhamma of the present moment! You're not accepting the reality that's right there in front of you. You begin judging and condemning, and, most often, blaming somebody else for, disturbing you.

Well, I'm sorry... They're *not* disturbing your practice. THEY ARE PART OF THE PRACTICE! There's no such thing as something else, or someone else, disturbing MY PRACTICE. It's only me fighting with what is real, the REALITY, the Dhamma of the present moment, not liking this or that, and next, I am blaming somebody else OR something else for the cause of that...

# CHAPTER FOURTEEN – Forgive it!

What about sounds disturbing us while we practice? Sometimes, in a retreat, if you are concentrating too hard you can observe what can happen. You could get SO upset if there is even one squeak of a door, or someone is walking by too heavily near you, or breathing too loudly. You might jump up thinking "OH! You disturbed my practice!"

Do you begin to see how ridiculous this actually is? What is happening here is that the present moment produced a noise; and there was noise, and then, mind came up and said, "I don't like this. That's not supposed to be there." "I want to complain to somebody, and make them stop so MY mind can be peaceful!" What is actually happening is concentration is out of balance with mindfulness. Concentration is too strong and mindfulness is too weak. Hahaha! How crazy is that?

If you can't accept what's happening in the present moment, with a balanced mind, there will be suffering. OK! So! There's a noise. "There's somebody talking!" So? It doesn't matter just as long as you have mindfulness and equanimity in your mind. When balance is in your mind, if there is a noise, that's just fine. And? You can do your forgiveness meditation!

While I was in Asia on a three month retreat. There was a water well pump that was drilling for water right outside of the meditation hall. Three months of an old clanky motor running from 8 o'clock in the morning until 6 o'clock at night. This can happen, you know? One continuous noise! It was really loud and really annoying, but, it was just sound. That's all it was. I realized that it was not "MY" sound. "My" dislike of that sound wasn't going to change that sound. "My" criticizing of the person that started the motor wasn't going to make that sound any different.

Do you see where all the attachments are in this example? The exercise here is accepting the fact that sound is here, and it's ok for sound to be here. It has to be ok, because, that's what's in the present moment. That's the truth [Dhamma]. Accepting the present moment is accepting the Dhamma just as it is.

Whenever there is a disturbance, forgive the disturbance continually in your mind. FORGIVE. Smile. Forgive yourself for not understanding. That is how we work with forgiveness in daily life. I forgive myself for wanting things to be more perfect than they are. I forgive myself for making mistakes. I forgive myself for being angry, and, disliking this or that. Now we see that the forgiveness is not just one statement, it can be many. We take each of these statements into the practice and use them one by one.

# CHAPTER FIFTEEN – No Mantras

While you're doing your sitting practice, once again, you just want to take one statement of forgiveness at a time. Stay with just one. Remember that this is not a mantra. You don't surface say this and think about something else either. It has to be sincere. "I really do forgive myself for making mistakes or for not understanding or whatever". It's important to be sincere when you do this.

The more you can continually forgive, with your daily activities, with your sitting, with your walking meditation, whatever you happen to be doing; you need to realize that this is what meditation is really about.

Meditation is not about gaining some super-human state of mind. It's not just about bliss. It is more productive than that. It's about learning how you cause your own suffering and how to let go of that suffering. The deeper super-human states of meditation will come up by themselves when we clear our minds and simply allow this to happen. You don't have to personally do anything.

The more you clear yourself, the more you clear your mind of judgments, opinions, concepts, ideas, and the more

you accept what's happening in the present moment, the more joyful life becomes. The easier life becomes.

What's that you are saying now? "Well, I have this habit of always analyzing and thinking." OK, let it go. "BUT I have been doing this my whole life." So? Hey! Forgive yourself for not understanding. Forgive yourself for analyzing.

There can be a strong attachment to wanting to analyze. That's the Western disease. "I want to know how everything works." You don't learn how things work by thinking about them. You let go and relax to see how things work when you forgive, and, you let go and relax to develop space in your mind to observe how they work.

The truth is that, in meditation, thinking mind, analyzing mind is incredibly slow. The aware mind is incredibly fast. It's extraordinary! You just can't get there with a lot of words in the way. You can't have opinions in the way. They will block you. They will stop you from seeing the way things truly are.

# CHAPTER SIXTEEN – Blame Game

Your Forgiveness Meditation is more than just about old attachments like, "Well, when I was five years old, Little Johnny, he beat me up and I've hated him ever since then." See how this is about you and uncovering this attachment and how you hold onto it, and how you cause yourself pain because of that attachment?

Most especially these days, people are really big on blaming everybody but themselves for their pain, and, the question here should be, is that working with reality or not? It's easy to say, "YOU caused me pain. I don't like you." But, did someone else cause you pain? Or did I just say something and you had another kind of an opinion, and, judged and condemned whatever I said, and then, your aversion came up, and the dislike of the whole situation, and now, you're off to the races and you're a thousand miles away.

You are causing yourself pain and you're running into your thinking, "But, I'm only thinking and analyzing." Ha ha ha ha ha! You're attached! You think, "This attachment won't hurt me so much if I keep distracted. I can keep MY opinions, and my ideas about the way things are supposed to be, and then, I don't have to change!" But, you're fooling

yourself. Change is the only way to free mind. Meditation is about positive change.

# CHAPTER SEVENTEEN – Be Happy!

In summary, BUDDHISM is about realizing that you need to have a balanced and mindful mind, that doesn't have high emotions in it, that doesn't' have attachments in it, so that you can see things clearly and discover real happiness and contentment in daily life.

BUDDHISM is about seeing the way things truly are; gaining knowledge by seeing for yourself how you are the cause of your own pain. It's about taking personal responsibility and doing the work needed to find this kind of mindfulness, balance and understanding.

Mindfulness of Forgiveness Meditation trains us to recognize clearly when suffering arises [First Noble Truth]; to notice how we get personally involved with it and make it bigger which causes more suffering in life [Second Noble Truth]; and to escape this dangerous trap by using the 6R's and seeing how it disappears [Third Noble Truth]; This meditation opens the way for clear understanding and relief [Fourth Noble Truth].

The end-result creates the space we need in our mind so that we begin to respond to life instead of re-acting. Using the 6R's, which fulfills the practice of Right Effort found in

the early texts; using it with any meditation you are doing, this is one of the fastest ways for all people to see clearly what is really going on and to reach this kind of destination where there can be happiness and Peace.

In sutta number 21 of the Majjhima Nikaya, as translated by Bhikkhu Bodhi, within The Middle Length Sayings' and published by Wisdom Publications, it gives us some excellent advice that I would like to share with you now. It says:

"There are these five courses of speech that others may use when they address you, their speech may be timely or untimely, true or untrue, gentle or harsh, connected with good or connected with harm, spoken with a mind of loving-kindness or with inner hatred.

"This is how I should train: My mind shall be unaffected and I will utter no evil words; I shall abide compassionate for their welfare, with a mind of loving-kindness, without inner hate. I shall abide pervading that person (whoever you talk with) with a mind imbued with loving-kindness (and forgiveness) and starting with him, I shall abide pervading the all-encompassing world with a mind imbued with loving-kindness, abundant, exalted, immeasurable, without hostility and without ill-will". That is how I should train.

Please use this Forgiveness Meditation often and train your mind to be happy!

# APPENDIX 1 - Review of T.W.I.M.

A quick brush-up on:

"Simple, Easy to Understand Mindfulness"

"Tranquil Wisdom Insight Meditation" (TWIM) training is the basic framework for all of our meditation methods and their resultant success.

**MEDITATION** is "observing mind's attention as it moves moment-to-moment in order to see precisely 'HOW' suffering happens. Too understand this, we study the impersonal process of Human Cognition. This reveals HOW we experience our environment. Seeing and understanding 'HOW' mind' works when attention moves from one thing to another is what this ancient practice is about. This leads us to a more impersonal perspective so that we do not suffer so deeply while living life.

**MINDFULNESS** is what keeps this observation going all the time. Tranquil Wisdom Insight Meditation (TWIM) is a reclaimed ancient guidance system with 6 simple steps to keep our meditation going strong. Mindfulness helps us develop our observation skill so we can keep the 6R's going. Mindfulness tells us what to do. It helps us RECOGNIZE when tension changes in our bodies as mind's attention moves away from our object of meditation

or from our task in life. We REMEMBER [use mindfulness] to observe mind's attention moving and then the practice cycle can begin to help us make a correction and continue meditating. So, Mindfulness is the fuel just like gas keeps a car going. Without Mindfulness, everything stops! If we persistently keep going, the meditation will relieve suffering of all kinds. So, to begin the cycle "smoothly" one must start the engine and have lots of gas (mindfulness) in the tank! Now we continue on with the steps of the Meditation Cycle.

**RECOGNIZE**: This means we learn to recognize any movement of mind's attention away from an object of meditation, such as the breath, sending out of Metta, practicing Forgiveness or, any task in daily life that you are doing.

We can learn to notice a slightly tense sensation as mind's attention barely begins to move toward an arising phenomena. Pleasant or painful feeling can occur at any one of the six sense doors. Any sight, sound, odor, taste, touch, or thought can cause a pulling sensation to begin. With careful non-judgmental observation, the meditator notices a slight tightening sensation. Watch carefully. RECOGNIZING this early movement is vital to successful meditation. One then continues on to...

**RELEASE**: When a thought or feeling arises, the meditator RELEASES it, let's it be there without giving any more attention to it. We do not feed it attention. The content of the distraction is not important at all, but the mechanics of HOW it arose **ARE** important! Just let go of any tightening around it. Let it be there without placing attention on it. Without attention, the tightness will pass

away.  Then Mindfulness reminds the meditator to...

RELAX: After releasing the feeling or sensation, and allowing it to be there without trying to control it, there is a subtle, barely noticeable tension in mind/body. This is why the extra TRANQUILIZATION] or RELAX step is being pointed out in the Buddha's instructions.  It turns out that within the Ānāpānasati instructions, the tranquilization step mentioned was a separate independent step.  Over time this instruction has become blurred.

## PLEASE, DON'T SKIP THIS STEP!

A motor can't run smoothly without oil in the engine. This is the oil! Without performing this relaxation step every time in the practice cycle, the meditator will not experience the reality of the state of cessation of suffering as a real state.  The tension was caused by CRAVING and this cuts us off from discovering a ceasing of the suffering.  We cannot feel the relief when the tightness falls away if we do not perform this relax step. This is cutting edge.

Note: ***Craving always manifests as a tightness or tension in both one's mind and body.***

One has a momentary opportunity to see and experience the true nature and relief that comes from cessation of the tightness within suffering while performing the RELEASE/RELAX steps. Notice this relief.  Mindfulness now reminds us to...

RE-SMILE: If you have listened to the meditation instructions at our website you might remember hearing how smiling is an important aspect for this meditation. Smiling in your mind, in your eyes, in your heart, and on your

lips helps sharpen awareness, become alert, agile and more observant. Getting serious, tensing up or frowning causes mind to become heavy, dull and slow. Mindfulness falls down. Insights become difficult to experience. This slows understanding the truth of HOW things work. So, Re-smile. Start again. Keeping up your humor, sense of fun, and exploration is important. After re-smiling, mindfulness recalls the next step...

**RETURN or RE-DIRECT**: Gently re-direct mind's attention back to the object of meditation that is the **breath and relaxing**, or **metta and relaxing**. Continue on with a gentle collected mind and use your object of meditation as a "home base", a re-centering point during the practice. This will help you stay in the present moment in daily life. If you are pulled off task, one returns mind's attention back to releasing, relaxing, and re-smiling into whatever task you are doing in life.

Imagine, for a moment, you are a resting under an Apple Tree, not serious and tense about anything. As you lean back against the tree, not thinking about anything, you attain a pleasant abiding with a light mind. This is what first happened to the Buddha when he was very young while sitting under a Rose-Apple Tree during a Harvest Festival his Father was attending.

Want to see things more clearly? Be still. Lighten up. SMILE. This opens the door to a happier life. If you forget to Release/Relax, don't punish yourself. Instead of punishing or criticizing yourself, be kind and forgive yourself.

Sometimes people say this practice cycle is simpler than expected! Reclaiming this practice develops more effective focus for daily tasks, more balance, deeper sleep, and people become more easy going and happy. The

meditator becomes more efficient at whatever they are doing in life. Because they discover more about HOW things actually work, this helps them to have less fear and hesitation in life.    Mindfulness then helps with a final recollection to...

REPEAT:  this practice cycle to retrain mind to relieve suffering in this lifetime. Repeating the "6R's cycle" over and over again trains mind to let go of a lot of suffering as we realize the meaning of the Four Noble Truths

1) We see and experience for ourselves what suffering actually is [First Noble Truth];

2) We notice the cause which is becoming personally involved it causing  tension and tightness [Second Noble Truth];

3) We experience what the cessation of suffering feels like [Third Noble Truth]; and

4) We discover a way to increase this comfortable state of the cessation of suffering. [Fourth Noble Truth].

This happens each time we Release an arising feeling, Relax and Re-smile.  Notice the Relief. Keep it going and give your smiles away!   That is the entire practice in a nutshell. Now go for it!

# *About the Author*

The principle guiding Teacher is our Abbot Most Venerable "Bhante" Vimalaramsi

Mahāthera; Trained through the Burmese Theravāda School and Mahāsi System of training. But now a declared Suttavadin!

Founder: United International Buddha Dhamma Society 2003, Abbot for Dhamma Sukha Meditation Center/ Anāthapiṇḍika's Study Park Complex 2005-Present, Official Founder and Spiritual head for the Buddhist American Forest Tradition (New Suttavada Sect). Bhante is Head Teacher for Tranquil Wisdom Insight Meditation and he oversees the research, practice, preservation, and teaching of early foundation Buddhist teachings as found in the Pali texts.

He has been a monk since 1986, with over 40 years of practice and with over 12 years of that in Asia. He holds the first life-time position given to a Representative for Buddhists in the USA; to the World Buddhist Council based in Kobe, Japan. 2006 - Questions may be sent to Bhante Vimalaramsi via info@dhammasukha.org

# *Other Resources*

Dhamma Sukha Meditation Center website:
www.dhammasukha.org.

Vimalaramsi, Bhante, *Meditation is Life, Life is Meditation* (CreateSpace, 2014).

Vimalaramsi, Bhante, *Breath of Love* (Ehipassiko Foundation of Indonesia, 2012).

Vimalaramsi, Bhante, *Moving Dhamma, Volume 1.* (CreateSpace, 2012).


Dhamma Sukha Meditation Center

8218 County Road 204

Annapolis, MO 63620

info@dhammasukha.org

# *Sharing Merit*

May Suffering ones by suffering free
and the fear-struck, fearless be,
May the grieving shed all grief,
and may all beings find relief.

May all beings share this merit that we have thus acquired,
for the acquisition of all kinds of happiness.
May beings inhabiting Space and Earth,
Devas and Nagas of mighty power,
share this merit of ours.

May they long protect the Buddha's Dispensation.

SADHU, SADHU, SADHU

CPSIA information can be obtained
at www.ICGtesting.com
Printed in the USA
BVOW03s1232301217
503281BV00021B/83/P